A HISTORY OF THE
END OF THE WORLD

A HISTORY OF THE
END OF THE WORLD

OVER 80 TALES OF ARMAGEDDON AND GLOBAL EXTINCTION
FROM ANCIENT BELIEFS TO PROPHECIES AND SCIENTIFIC PREDICTIONS

TIM RAYBORN

CIDER MILL
PRESS

BOOK
PUBLISHERS
KENNEBUNKPORT, MAINE

CONTENTS

CHAPTER 2: SCIENCE

CHAPTER 3: CONSPIRACIES, SUPERSTITIONS, AND FAILED PREDICTIONS

CHAPTER 4: LITERATURE AND POP CULTURE

INTRODUCTION

THE END OF THE WORLD is a big deal.

And not just because it's the end of the world.

For as long as humanity has been around, people have wondered who they are, where they come from, and where they're going. They've tried to answer them using myth, religion, philosophy, art, and more recently, science.

We're still far from having all the answers. But one thing we can be sure of: countless people have wondered what might become of the world we live in. Will it always be here? Or will something make it all go away some day? Religion, various myths, and science have stepped up to supply answers, and although they don't agree on the details, they do agree on one thing: one day, all of this will come to an end.

You've probably heard the words *apocalypse* and *Armageddon*. *Apocalypse* comes from the Greek word *apokalypsis*, which means "to uncover" or "to reveal." Originally, an "apocalypse" was a form of writing popular in the Middle East that tried to provide its readers comfort, grant them a sense of what was going to happen based around events from the present time. So it was "revealing" answers and hidden meanings. Nowadays, *apocalypse* usually means something that brings about the end of the world.

Armageddon comes from the Hebrew term, *har mĕgiddōn*, or "hill of Megiddo," a place where some Christians believe that the forces of evil will gather to wage war on the world at the end of time. This hill is an actual place, and is mentioned specifically in the Book of Revelation (16:16).

Although it's true that religions, especially those that originated in the Middle East, have very detailed descriptions of what they believe will happen at the end, there are stories from all over the world about the events that will bring us to our doom. From Scandinavia and Africa to Central America and Asia, people both ancient and modern have wondered and worried about the day no one wants to be around to experience.

But predictions about that last day are not limited to religion and myth. Scientists have been hard at work over the years figuring out ways that our tiny, fragile little planet could fail, or be destroyed. And they have come up with quite a few that are not only frightening, but frighteningly possible, even in your lifetimes!

This inclination to speculate about the world's end has also spurred some people to come up with their own ideas about what might happen. Some of these stories might seem reasonable, but others are just downright weird and wild! Groups of people have even gathered into cults and secret societies because of their powerful belief in a specific set of bizarre apocalyptic theories. Many of these sects have made fantastic predictions about the end of the world, but at present, all have failed to come true.

The ultimate end has become so embedded in the cultural conversation that a huge number of people love to be entertained by ideas of the world ending in science fiction and horror novels, movies, TV shows, video games, and other forms of media. Maybe they make the idea easier for us to understand and accept. Or maybe we just like being scared!

The entries in this book provide a good introduction to how many different ways humanity has come up with to imagine its end, the world's end, and even the universe's end. Some are weirder than others, but they all tug at us a little. They reside at the backs of our minds, making us a little bit excited, and a little bit anxious, occasionally keeping us awake as we lie in bed, wondering what we're moving toward.

CHAPTER 1
RELIGION AND MYTH

HUMANS HAVE ALWAYS WONDERED about where they come from and where they're going. Why are we here? Are we a product of the natural world, or were we created? If so, by whom? What happens when we die? And what will happen to this world we live in?

You're probably not surprised to learn that there are many speculations about the possible end of the world, coming from cultures all around the globe. But not every religion has a belief in the end of the world, and, for some that do, it's not the fiery, deadly apocalypse that we have heard about. Some cultures even believed that the end of the world *already happened*, and we are living in what came after!

Here is a collection of religious beliefs, myths, and folktales about what might await us, or the very distant future. From the familiar story of the final judgment to the violent war in the Ragnarök myth; from the inescapable cycles of the Greek philosophers and Asian sages to the ominous signs present in Native American lore, here is a treasury of end-of-the-world stories from the world's many beliefs and traditions.

RAGNARÖK

ONE OF THE MOST FAMOUS of all mythological stories about the end of the world, Ragnarök ("the fate of the gods") is the end of all things predicted in Norse and Icelandic myth. It's not clear when belief in this violent and detailed vision of the end of the world first took hold, but by the time of the Vikings (the ninth and tenth centuries), it seems to have been well known.

The story of Ragnarök, like many of the Norse myths, is told in the poetic and prose *Edda* of medieval Iceland (twelfth and thirteenth centuries), collected and recorded by Icelandic poet and historian Snorri Sturluson (1179-1241). By that time, much of Iceland's population was Christian, but some likely still held on to the older religion, and still feared the fate that awaited them.

The gods themselves know what is to come, and try as they might, they cannot stop it from happening. The *Edda* stories say that prior to the end of the world, there would be three straight years of fierce winter on Earth. This is the warning sign that the final war is about to start. The battle will be fought between the Norse gods, led by Odin, and the Jötnar (giants) and other foes, led by the trickster Loki and Surtr the fire giant. The giants have long been the enemies of the gods and have tried to destroy them. This time, they will succeed.

In this great battle, heroic gods will face off against various monsters, but they won't survive. Odin is fated to meet the giant wolf Fenrir, who will swallow him whole. Odin's son, Vidar, will kill Fenrir in revenge. Thor will fight the dreaded Midgard Serpent (a gigantic snake that circles the whole world). He will kill the beast, but the serpent's deadly venom will in turn kill Thor. The god Heimdall will kill Loki, who will kill him in turn. After this great battle has taken down many of the gods, Surtr will set the whole world on fire, destroying everything.

But this is not the absolute end. Some gods will survive: Thor's sons, Odin's son Baldr, and various others will take up places in the new cosmos that rises from the ashes of the old. Two humans will also survive and repopulate this new world so that the cycle can begin again.

It's possible that some of Ragnarök was an interpretation of Christian beliefs about the end of the world. We'll never know for sure, because these stories were only written down after the age of the Vikings had ended. But this bleak and frightening set of myths probably tells us something about the Norse people who believed in them and the oft harsh and cold world they lived in, suggesting a belief in fate so strong that even the gods couldn't escape.

THE CELTS

CELTIC IS A TRICKY TERM THESE DAYS. A lot of people cannot seem to agree on what it means, or who it refers to. In modern times, we usually think of people from Ireland, Scotland, and Wales when we hear the term, but *Celtic* applies to a wider swath of the world than just those three countries. It comes from the ancient Greek word *keltoi*, which simply meant "barbarians," aka anyone who, in the opinion of the Greeks, was not Greek! Tribes that have been identified as "Celtic" lived as far away as modern Turkey, as well as in Switzerland and northern Spain.

The Celts in Gaul (modern-day France) gave Julius Caesar a very hard time, and he wrote about his military campaigns against them. They were famed for their beautiful metalwork, and for being fearless in battle, a courage that seems to be fostered by a frequently held belief in reincarnation. If they were to be reborn, why should they fear rushing into battle against the Romans?

These Celts relied on the wisdom of the Druids, who were a class of teachers, scholars, poets, judges, and possibly priests, that were at the heart and soul of Celtic society.

For this entry, let's talk about the Celts of Gaul and the British Isles as they were during the time of the Roman Empire, and after it. Did these peoples have anything like Ragnarök, a vast, destructive myth about the end of the world? Not that we know of, at least not anything that has survived in writing.

But one apocalyptic-tinged Celtic myth was written down in the eleventh or twelfth centuries that copied text from the ninth century: "The Second Battle of Mag Tuired."

At the end of the second battle, Morrigan, the goddess of war and destiny, makes an ominous prediction about the times to come. She says that she foresees an era when the world will no longer be dear to her. It will be an age when summer will bring no growth, when cows will no longer give milk, and when people will live without honor. People will lie and betray one another, children will deceive their parents, and lawlessness and disease will abound.

Morrigan doesn't say what will happen next (or maybe she did, in a piece of text that didn't survive), but it is clear that this is a dangerous time, taking humanity and the world in a direction it may never be able to find its way back from. This myth contains a lesson that's still valuable: if we're not careful, every age is potentially the final one.

Because this prediction was written down long after most of the Celts became Christian, we cannot be sure if it is an ancient prophecy, or one that was influenced by Christian teachings later on. But obviously, someone thought it was important.

THE BOOK OF REVELATION

FOR CHRISTIANS, this apocalyptic story is the most famous of all, foretelling a time of great conflict and destruction that results in the end of the world, the return of Christ, the forces of evil being defeated once and for all, the arrival of Judgment Day, and, finally, the blessed getting to live forever in glory. Written in the later first century, allegedly by a man named John of Patmos, it is the final book of the Bible, and a work that has confused, confounded, and frightened Christians ever since.

It tells of angels opening seals and sounding trumpets, and then destruction raining down on Earth. It warns of the dreaded Four Horsemen: war, famine, plague, and death riding over the world and bringing chaos and ruin with them. There is a Beast, whose number is 666, who will deceive the people. There will be a final battle between the forces of good and evil, and a divine judgment. Those who are vindicated by this judgment will live forever, while the sinners who fail will be cast into a lake of fire to be tormented forever.

It's frightening stuff and, as you might expect, has been a source of controversy for as long as it has existed. Although many have tried to predict when these dreaded last days would come (you'll read about some of these instances in Chapter 3), others have warned that it was not for us to know the date and time, that the end would catch us by surprise. Still, over the centuries, many have looked at the issues plaguing their own times and believed they provided evidence that the end was approaching fast. But what was this story, really?

These types of writings, known as apocalypses, were actually common in the ancient world. Revelation takes images and ideas from the Old Testament's Book of Daniel, a look back because Christians in the late first century were experiencing something similar to the Jews from several hundred years earlier, when the Babylonian Empire conquered Israel and sent its people into slavery. Daniel told of the sorrow this caused. At the time Revelation was written, the Romans were persecuting Christians throughout their empire. Thus, Rome was the "new Babylon," and would eventually fail. The Beast was the Roman emperor, and the wars, disease, famine, and death were things that happened because of misguided Roman policies.

The text was really encouraging its readers to stay strong, because eventually they would win out. But why did so many people think it predicted the end of the world? Well, over time, as Christianity spread farther and farther away from Jerusalem, Christians were not as familiar with the story told in Daniel. When these folks read Revelation, they speculated about what it meant.

By the beginning of the fourth century, when Christianity had spread far and wide and the Bible took on its final form, Revelation was adapted to this broader outlook and took on a very different meaning than it had for the early Christians in Jerusalem. What had started as an attempt to look back to the past and make readers feel better became something scary, about a far-in-the-future time, likely far from what the original author had likely intended.

JUDAISM

IN TRADITIONAL JEWISH BELIEF, the end is more about setting things right in this world.

An important part of Jewish tradition is the belief that the Messiah will come and restore the world to right after Israel has been reestablished. Obviously, for Christians, Jesus was the Messiah, but the Jews rejected this. For them, Jesus is just another in a long line of prophets, not the promised ruler who would bring peace.

For most Jewish traditions, the Messiah is an earthly ruler who will bring justice and peace to the whole world and whose reign will be long—maybe even for thousands of years. All will be well, no war or disease, and even animals will not fight each other. As you can imagine, a lot of people over the centuries have been proposed to be this person, and at least as many have claimed to be the Messiah. But all of them have failed to deliver on the glorious promise that Jews have for this individual.

As with Christians and other groups when describing the approaching end times, Jews believe that numerous signs will foretell the coming of the Messiah: troubles, wars, violence, hatred, evil, and so on. Of course, these things have been part of humanity for as long as we've been here, so it's only natural that at any time, people could look at the world and see evidence that the end *must* be coming soon.

For some Jews, the loss of Israel to the Romans in the first century, and then its reappearance in the 1940s as a new, modern nation is all the proof they need that the time of the Messiah is drawing near. Others simply say that only God knows when this time will arrive, and that it is not for humans to try to guess when it will be.

ISLAM

ISLAM, LIKE CHRISTIANITY, looks back to Jewish sources for many of its core beliefs, and the three religions all share the same first prophet: Abraham. Islam holds that Judaism and Christianity are legitimate religions from God, but they have picked up mistakes and errors along the way, which Islam was sent to correct. Because Muslims see themselves as coming out of the same traditions, it's only natural that there would be an Islamic belief in the end of the world, too. There are two main branches of Islam, Sunni and Shia, and both believe that the end of the world will come eventually. Because the Sunni branch is by far the larger of these two, we'll focus on their beliefs.

In the Sunni tradition, Jesus is not the son of God, but rather a great prophet who is worthy of respect and admiration (though not worship). There will be a Judgment Day in the future, and the dead will rise from their graves to be judged for their deeds in life. Many Muslims believe that Jesus will return, but not to be proclaimed as the King of Kings and the incarnation of God. Rather, he will remove the errors from the beliefs of the Christians and judge those who have done wrong and evil.

Before this judgment, there will be a time of great trials and suffering on Earth. A figure known as Dajjal will appear in the world (some see Dajjal as a concept rather than an individual, one that could refer to a time when things get really bad for humanity). At some point, the Kaaba (the most sacred place in Islam, located in the city of Mecca in Saudi Arabia) will be destroyed. After that, the *Dābbat al-Arḍ*, or "Beast of the Earth," will appear, and will speak harshly to the unbelievers of the world. Smoke will then cover Earth for many days, and earthquakes will shake the entire planet.

A wind will blow across the world, clearing the smoke, but also killing all the faithful Muslims. Those who do not believe will be left alive and face still greater suffering for the next 120 years. Then, the sun will rise in the west, a final trumpet will be blown, and all remaining people on Earth will die. Thereafter, the dead will be resurrected and brought to face their judgment.

The Qur'an, the holy book of Islam, says that anyone who has done good and right in the world may be allowed to enter Jannah, or "Paradise," while the wicked and evil, no matter what other behavior they exhibited, will go to Jahannam, the place of punishment and torment.

The other main branch of Islam, the Shia, has end-of-the-world beliefs similar to those of the Sunni. But there are some differences, such as the belief in many hells and that souls might wait in either paradise or hell until the Day of Judgment.

THE YEAR 1000

IN THE BIBLE IT IS CLAIMED that the devil would be bound for 1,000 years and then be let loose to cause destruction on Earth. It would make sense, then, that the time of this binding would be in the aftermath of Christ being on Earth, and that, as the year 1000 dawned, things might get really bad, really quickly.

So, you might think that during the year 999, people started to get very nervous. And, many history books written in the centuries following the first millennium describe that time as one when people were panicking, getting upset, and doing crazy things, all out of fear of what would soon happen. There are stories of people selling or giving away all their possessions, of crazed hermits preaching to large crowds, demanding that they repent, of people going crazy with fear and committing violence. According to some, whole towns were abandoned, buildings fell into ruin, mobs attacked the innocent, and people went on long and painful pilgrimages in an effort to obtain forgiveness for their sins. These behaviors only got worse as 999 rolled on, and when the New Year finally came and nothing happened, some people were relieved, and some were embarrassed for how they'd acted. This was the popular view for a long time, and it seemed very reasonable, given people's fears and superstitions.

One problem: When historians started taking a closer look at the writings from the time, they found very little evidence that any of this crazy behavior had happened, or if it had, it was in very small groups and outbreaks. There was no mass panic, no signs of civilization breaking down. People who were conscious of the devilish significance of the date (and that wouldn't have been everyone), might have been bothered by it, but it seems most took their own precautions and waited to see. Some councils of church leaders met to discuss the issue, so there's no doubt the date was significant to some. But there doesn't seem to have been anything resembling the widespread panic many historians set down.

Or maybe, when the year came and went and nothing apocalyptic happened (per usual), those who had lost their minds were so embarrassed about their behavior that they destroyed any record of it, or refused to write it down and expose themselves!

HINDUISM: THE KALI YUGA

IN THE INDIAN RELIGION of Hinduism, the Kali Yuga is the last of the four ages (*yugas*) of the universe. Before the Kali Yuga, there were the Satya/Krita Yuga, Treta Yuga, and Dvapara Yuga. Yugas are

immensely long time periods, and though we live in the Kali Yuga now (it began about 5,000 years ago), it will not end for more than 426,000 years! So, if you're one of those who're worried about the world coming to an end soon, Hinduism's here to reassure you that it's gonna be a bit.

This last age is ruled by the demon Kali, who has the same name as the great goddess Kali. The goddess Kali, though fearsome looking, destroys evil, whereas the demon Kali wants to encourage it and destroy the world. The demon Kali is opposed by Kalki, who is the god Vishnu in human form (avatar). When Kalki is born at the end of the Kali Yuga, he will set about making everything right again.

Before this time, things will be bad, and gradually get much worse: crime will increase; murder and war will become general; people will become more deceptive and greedier, and cheat each other for personal gain; leaders will become tyrannical, oppressing their people and becoming a threat to all; the rich will dominate and harm the poor; and lies will spread easily and, worse, be believed by most people.

There will be problems with the natural world as well: the weather will become more unstable; the environment will get worse; there will be many earthquakes; and disease will spread throughout the world.

You may be thinking: these things are already happening. That's a big part of understanding the Kali Yuga. These problems *are* already happening, but belief in this final age says that they are only going to get worse over thousands and thousands of years. So, you might think of this as a commentary on the problems human society will forever face, or it could be seen as a genuine prophecy of what is happening and what is going to happen.

And just what will happen? As in some other belief systems, this one is a cycle. As mentioned, at the very end of the Kali Yuga, Vishnu will return to Earth as Kalki, who will destroy evil, setting things right for the next cycle of Yugas to begin. We will leave this destructive time and enter a new golden age, and the cycle will continue, over and over, forever.

BUDDHISM

THERE ARE MANY DIFFERENT branches of Buddhism across Asia today, and all of them believe that an individual named Siddhartha, an Indian prince who lived more than 2,500 years ago, struck out to find the meaning of life after becoming disenchanted with his own existence. After trying everything he could think of over a span of many years, he finally sat under a tree and meditated deeply. Eventually, he achieved a state of enlightenment, or true knowledge, about the world and the universe. Afterward, he became known as the Buddha, or the "one who is awake," because he had "woken up" to the true nature of reality.

After this, he began to travel all across India, spreading his message and teaching others how to "wake up" as he had.

That is known to many. What is less familiar is that Buddhism has a concept of the end of the world, though it varies between the traditions. Some believe that the Buddha himself predicted the end of the world. Because nothing lasts forever, the Buddha is said to have foretold that the world itself would pass away, over the course of thousands of years. The end will begin when a second sun appears and starts to dry up the land. Then a third sun will arrive, doing still more damage. Seven suns will appear in total, and with the final sun, Earth will burn up. Some have noticed that this process seems very similar to what scientists think will happen with our own sun as it grows larger and larger over billions of years, until it eventually absorbs Earth.

Another branch of Buddhism predicts the appearance of Maitreya. According to this teaching, about 5,000 years after the Buddha lived, all Buddhist teachings will be forgotten, and the world will fall into hopelessness and evil. But a new Buddha, Maitreya, will be born and bring people back to goodness and justice. Sometime after that, the world will either end or enter a new cycle.

MESOPOTAMIAN MYTHS

THE GREAT MYTHS of the Sumerians and Babylonians are some of the world's most intriguing stories. Thousands of years old, they were attempts by these early civilizations to make sense of a world that was mysterious, unpredictable, and violent. These stories told of order being made out of chaos, of violent clashes between gods and monsters, and the attempt to set the world right by creating humans to serve the gods. These inventions undoubtedly had an influence on later stories, such as those told in the Bible.

Mesopotamian cultures were less concerned about an upcoming end of the world than they were about the one that had already happened. They believed that at one time, the world had been destroyed by a great flood. There are various versions of the flood story, but the main idea was that the gods would, from time to time, worry that humanity was getting too overpopulated, or too disordered to carry out their true purpose: serving the gods to make their existence easier. This servitude was seen as the aim of everyone's existence, from farmers in the fields to priests and kings.

But sometimes, things went awry, and the gods decided to take action. Sometimes a god, such as Enlil (god of wind and storms), would send a famine or plague to take out some of the human population. Or would withhold life-giving water during a drought. Once, a vast flood destroyed everything and everyone, except for Atrahasis, who was able to escape after being warned by the god Enki (god of water and knowledge). Atrahasis was later able to make peace with the gods through offerings, and the human race was allowed to start over again. In another version of the myth, King Ziusudra (or Zi-ud-sura), the ruler of Shuruppak, built a boat after receiving a warning of the coming flood. After floating on stormy waters for seven days, the king was able to land and make an offering that appeased the gods.

The message in these stories is that humans must know their place. Otherwise, the gods would withdraw their favor, decide that they'd had enough, and eliminate civilization, leaving only a few to painstakingly make amends and piece society back together. Building a tradition around the concept of arbitrary destruction might seem unsettling to us, but to an ancient people trying to make sense of a world where natural disasters and disease arrived without warning, it must have been a reminder of all that remained out of their control.

THE ZOROASTRIAN RENEWAL OF THE COSMOS

ZOROASTRIANISM IS AN ANCIENT Middle Eastern religion that originated in Iran. It may be well more than 3,000 years old, but first reports of the religion appear in the fifth century BCE. Based on the works and sayings of a spiritual teacher named Zoroaster (also known as Zarathustra), the religion worshipped a great god of good named Ahura

Mazda, or "Wise Lord." Ahura Mazda is opposed by Angra Mainyu, the destructive spirit. These two are in eternal conflict, and humanity's goal is to side with the forces of good, and to reject evil.

Zoroastrianism had a definite influence on other religions in the Middle East and beyond, including Christianity and Islam, as well as Greek philosophy and possibly even Buddhism. Though it has gone through many changes over thousands of years, many still follow it today, with the majority of those present followers residing in India.

It may have been one of the first known religions to form the concept of the end of the world. Zoroastrians came to believe in the *Frashokereti*, or "renewal of the universe," a time when evil would be overcome and purged from the world. They had several ideas at the core of these beliefs:

- The world is basically good, but has become corrupted over time by evil.
- Good will eventually win over evil.
- The world will be restored to the way it was.
- Each person is responsible for their own behavior and the outcome for themselves at that time.

The end will come at the "third time," which is the time of separation. The first two times were those of creation and mixing together. In this last age, the forces of good will battle the forces of evil, and the dead will be resurrected. The dead will then be put through judgment. Molten metal will be poured over the earth and all, both living and dead, will be required to walk through it, as if wading in shallow water. Those who are good and have lived lives of honor and kindness will be able to walk through the metal as if it were warm milk. But those who are evil, who have caused harm and who have sinned, will be burned up and destroyed.

The metal will then flow down to destroy Angra Mainyu and the forces of evil once and for all. Some among later Zoroastrians who believed that the evil individuals who were burned by the metal would in fact be purified by it, not destroyed. Thus there was hope for everyone to be redeemed. After that, the good will become immortal, Earth will become a paradise, and peace will reign.

It's obvious that some of these ideas found their way into other belief systems—their optimistic tone helps us understand why they spread far beyond Iran!

DAHĀG, THE THREE-HEADED IRANIAN DRAGON

OVERLAPPING WITH ZOROASTRIAN BELIEFS is the legend of Dahāg, or Zahhak, an evil creature in Persian mythology that causes much trouble and suffering. Dahāg is a monster, described as either a dragon or a human. As a dragon, he has three heads, and is fierce and terrifying. He is an ally of Angra Mainyu and an enemy of Ahura Mazda.

He was said to be the son of a ruler in Arabia (who Dahāg killed by tricking him into falling into a pit), and in time became a ruler himself, and a terrible one at that. He was advised by Angra Mainyu, and it was said that snakes grew from his face—snakes that demanded human brains every day to eat! He continued to rule in this way for centuries, until a young man named Fereydun decided to end his reign forever. The man-snake-dragon had tried to have Fereydun killed when he was only a boy, but failed, and now Fereydun was ready to bring the monster to justice.

Eventually, Fereydun fought against and defeated Dahāg. Some stories say that he killed the creature, but others say that when Dahāg was wounded, scorpions crawled out from his wounds and threatened to overrun the world, which would have made for a completely different spin on the end-of-the-world story.

To avoid this, Fereydun had the monster imprisoned underneath Mount Damavand, the tallest volcano in the land. And there he waits, trapped, but unable to do any more harm—until the end, of course. Legend says that in the last days, Dahāg will break free and rampage across the world, killing and eating at least a third of humanity. Eventually, another hero, named Kirsasp, will step in to finish the job once and for all, though not before the three-headed dragon causes much suffering and misery worldwide.

So, though Dahāg does not cause the end of the world, he will be one of its most terrifying sights when it approaches.

EGYPTIAN GOD ATUM

ANCIENT EGYPT HAD ONE of the most complex, amazing, and mysterious religions of any culture. Thousands of years later, it still proves fascinating. Much of it was concerned with preparing the soul for the afterlife. Elaborate rituals and spells were created to make sure that a person's spirit could find its way to where it would be able to live forever. This was especially true of the pharaohs, whose huge tombs were stuffed with just about every provision you can imagine, from clothing to jewelry to food and furniture.

The Egyptians believed in many gods, some of whom you probably know: Ra, Osiris, Isis, Horus, etc. But there were many more than these famous figures, including one of the more important earlier gods: Atum. For the Egyptians, Atum was not only the creator of the universe, he also kept it going. And, when the time was right, he would destroy it.

Atum was believed to have created himself from a mound of earth, known as Nun (nothing). He opened his mouth and out came Shu (air) and Tefnut (moisture), whom he later tabbed Life and Order, respectively. These two then gave birth to Geb (earth) and Nut (sky), and in turn these two produced the gods that are better known today. And so the universe was created, along with all the gods, Earth, creatures, and humanity. It was the duty of humans to honor the gods and act in good and just ways. If they failed, their souls might never properly pass into the afterlife, and would instead be devoured.

In the famed *Book of the Dead* (which gives instructions for how to prepare for the afterlife), Atum tells Osiris that he will eventually destroy everything, causing it to sink back into Nun, the great nothing there at the beginning of time. No one will survive, Atum says, except for the two of them, and he will live on in the form of a serpent.

So, when would this destruction occur? The time cycle will be millions of years, according to the *Book of the Dead*. So in reality, us mere mortals probably wouldn't be around to see it, anyway. Atum is clear that it will happen at some point, but it seems that the ancient Egyptians didn't live in constant fear of him bringing the world to an end on a whim, and didn't try to envision what form his annihilation would take.

UNIVERSAL FLOOD MYTHS

MOST ARE FAMILIAR WITH THE STORY of Noah and the Flood from the Book of Genesis, but it might surprise you to know that this famous apocalyptic story has many versions around the world. In some, the deluge is not caused by rain.

The most famous version outside of the one in the Bible is probably the story of Utnapishtim, from the Sumerian *Epic of Gilgamesh*. In it, the gods were angry with humanity and decided to destroy everyone with water. But the god Ea, or Enki, told one man, Utnapishtim, and instructed him to build a large boat to escape the coming flood with his wife. Utnapishtim does as told and prepares for the terrible and violent storm. As it rages, it is so awful it even frightens some of the gods, who begin to regret their decision as floodwaters pour over the world and destroy humanity. The storm keeps up for six days and six nights, and on the seventh day, there is calm. The boat lands on Mount Nimush, and Utnapishtim releases birds to go and find land. Afterward, when the gods learn that two humans have escaped the destruction, they are angry, but eventually, Utnapishtim and his wife are rewarded for their bravery and become gods.

In other parts of the world, there are equally dramatic flood stories. In Central America, flood myths have obviously been influenced by Christianity. But some are also very different, such as an Aztec myth where a man and woman survive the deluge and begin to cook a fish, only for the smoke from their cooking to give away that they are still alive. The gods are angry at this and turn them into dogs or monkeys, depending on the version you encounter!

Native Americans also use this trope to envision the world's potential end. In the Cree take on the tale, Wisagatcak the Trickster wants to capture the Great Beaver, and builds a dam over a river, intending to spear him as he floats by. But the Great Beaver is too clever, and as he floats by, he has a muskrat bite Wisagatcak on the behind, ruining the Trickster's chances of ensnaring him! Despite escaping, the Great Beaver is angry and wants revenge. Wisagatcak removes his dam, but the water level does not go down; instead, it keeps rising. And rising. Eventually, the water covers the whole world, with a group of animals riding a raft to safety.

What are these stories, really? There have been many theories. Some have suggested that Earth was struck by an asteroid or comet about 12,000 years ago, and it landed in an ocean, causing unimaginable flooding and damage worldwide. These myths may be a shadowy representation of that awful event, preserved by different peoples around the world. Others feel that these stories could be a way to foster the proper respect for the terrible power of the natural world.

But, given that humans need to live near a water source, floods are unavoidable, whether from heavy rain, snow melting, overflowing rivers, or other causes. Sometimes, these floods can devastate large areas. So, it follows that most cultures would have some myth about a great flood—whether these represent an actual historical event that affected the entire globe remains up for debate.

ENDS OF THE WORLD IN ANCIENT GREECE

YES, ENDS. The Greeks didn't believe in one specific time in the future when the world or the cosmos would come to an end at the hand of the angry gods. Instead, they believed that it had already happened. Three times! The gods had already grown disenchanted enough with humanity to destroy everyone in three great floods (there's that flood myth again!):

The time of King Ogyges: This first flood happened during the reign of Ogyges, the mythical king of Attica. Legends say that the flood was so damaging that Attica had no other king for a very long time.

The Deucalion legend: This story is similar to the tale of Noah and the ark, and the flood myth in the Sumerian *Epic of Gilgamesh*. It's said that the gods were ready to destroy the world with a flood and knowing this, the Titan Prometheus told his son, Deucalion, to build a chest. When the rains and waters came, everyone that wasn't high up in the mountains perished. Deucalion and his wife, Pyrrha, hid in the chest and floated on the waters for nine days before landing on Mount Parnassus, a mountain in central Greece.

Another version had the couple land in southern Greece, where Deucalion gave thanks to the god Zeus for being spared. Zeus instructed the couple to throw stones behind them. The ones that Deucalion threw became men, while the ones that Pyrrha threw became women, and so was Earth repopulated with humans.

The story of Dardanus: Dardanus, son of Zeus and Electra, left his home to make a new dwelling in the north. When the floods came again (those angry gods!), he and his family escaped, sailing east, where they were able to live on high ground for fifty years. Dardanus's son Tros was eventually able to move down to a plain, and there, on the shores of the sea, he founded a new city—Troy, which became one of the most famous cities of the ancient world.

These stories were known by many and served as reminders that humanity was always at the mercy of the whims of the gods. No one seemed to feel that there was a serious threat of a fourth flood, but these myths helped the Greeks understand that it couldn't be ruled out, either.

THE UNIVERSAL CYCLES OF THE STOICS

THE STOICS WERE A GROUP of ancient Greek philosophers, founded by a philosopher named Zeno of Citium about 2,300 years ago. They believed that true happiness (*eudaimonia*) came from accepting what was happening in the moment. How you acted and lived your life was the key to feeling happy and being at peace. Things like money, health, and pleasure were not good or bad by themselves; your relationship to them made the difference. As such, Stoics felt everyone should develop self-control to keep the bad and destructive emotions related to everyday existence at bay.

This was a very popular belief that remained in favor for hundreds of years, into the time of the Roman Empire. In fact, the Roman emperor Marcus Aurelius (second century) was a Stoic, and he wrote an important book about his beliefs, *Meditations*.

The Stoics had an unusual theory about the end of the world, one that resembles Hindu beliefs. They thought that the universe was caught in a cycle. At the end of the cycle, the entire universe would be destroyed by a fire they called the *ekpyrosis*. But this wasn't the end of everything once and for all. After this happened, the universe would be reborn (the *apokatastasis*), and everything would begin again.

But here's the catch: in this new universe, everything that had happened before, all of history, would happen exactly the same way again. You would be born, live your life, and die exactly as you had before. And not just once, but millions of times! And your fate was to do this over and over again, forever. So, as you're reading this book, you've already done it an infinite number of times, even if you don't remember!

The Stoics claimed that there isn't anything we can do about this; it's the way that the universe works, so we may as well accept it, and focus on living our lives with virtue. Some people might object, "Well, if everything just happens over and over, why bother to do anything good? Why help people? I may as well just live for myself, since I've already done that before, anyway!"

This seems like a good argument against Stoic philosophy, but a Stoic would likely answer that it is in our nature to live in harmony with the world and the universe, because our fate to do the same things over and over indicates that we are an essential part of it. Hurting others or being selfish is not how we can best honor this esteemed position.

CHINA: LI HONG AND TAOISM

CHINA HAS A NUMBER OF RELIGIOUS and philosophical beliefs, one of the most important being Taoism (pronounced "Dow-izum"). It's a philosophy that is both simple and complex, focusing on living peacefully and in harmony with the natural world. The Tao is sometimes translated as the "Way," and to embrace it is to "go with the flow," and be at peace with everything around you.

That overview might make it seem a bit strange that Taoism has a belief in the end of the world, though it's not a view filled in fire and destruction. There was a long-held belief by many Taoists that the human world, with its governments, economies, and focus on wealth, had become corrupted. One Taoist holy book from the fifth century, *The Divine Incantations Scripture*, tells of an important person (later believed to be Li Hong, a seventh-century ruler during the Tang dynasty) who would return to help restore order when everything was going wrong. The world would be "destroyed" in the sense that the old way of doing things would end and a new, more just and fair system would take its place.

Interestingly, the book says that those who uphold Taoist beliefs will be helped by a supernatural army, who would oppose the "demon kind" that were helping evil people succeed in the besmirched world. In this way, the text does resemble other apocalypse stories, but it stops short of saying that the world will actually be annihilated. The end of the world meant an end to evil and corruption, which would be replaced by something better. But over time, that evil would creep back in, and would have to be defeated again. The best way to go about this: stick with Taoist beliefs.

THE DISAPPEARING SUN GODDESS

JAPAN HAD ITS OWN NATIVE BELIEFS long before Buddhism became a popular religion there over the course of the fifth and sixth centuries CE. Although there wasn't a big myth about the end of the world, there was one tale that told of the time the sun went away, an occurrence that imperiled everything.

As the story goes, Amaterasu, the sun goddess, became very offended by the behavior of her brother, the god of storms. While she was celebrating at a festival to honor the arrival of the season's first fruits, her stormy brother made a mess of everything: destroying the rice crops in the fields, and even the hall where Amaterasu is celebrating!

She decides that she has had enough of this and retreats to a cave, where she will no longer shine. This would be fine if it were just her, of course. But her retreat means that the world no longer has a sun, and that everything will soon begin to die! The other gods can't let this happen, so they meet to discuss what they will do about it.

In this instance, the gods don't want to destroy the world; they want to save it, which makes this story different from many others we've encountered. One of the gods, the "Dread Female of Heaven," has an idea: she lights a fire and does a bizarre dance around it to make the other gods laugh. They laugh so hard and so loudly that the Amaterasu becomes curious about what's going on. When she tries to sneak out of the cave and spy on what's happening, some of the other gods grab her and force her to go back to lighting up the world, saving everyone and everything.

AIDO HWEDO, THE DRAGON OF WEST AFRICA

THE FON PEOPLE OF WEST AFRICA have legends about a great dragon, Aido Hwedo. According to the story, the god Nana-Buluku wanted a companion, and thus fashioned the rainbow dragon, Aido Hwedo. Then Nana-Buluku created everything else with the help of the dragon. The movements the dragon made carved out the shape of Earth and populated it with new life: plants, then animals, and finally human beings.

There was so much in this world that Nana-Buluku feared it might not be able to bear the weight of it all. Aido Hwedo wanted to keep this from happening, so he formed his body into a circle (he had a very long neck and tail), and held his tail in his mouth. This circle fit around the whole world, allowing Aido Hwedo to hold everything together, and keep Earth from collapsing. But Aido Hwedo could not stand to be in the sunlight all the time, so Nana-Buluku created an ocean for the dragon to live in while he supported the world.

Aido Hwedo continues to carry this burden to this very day. He is fed by monkeys who swim into the sea and give him iron bars to eat, keeping him full and content. But if the monkeys ever run out of iron bars, Aido Hwedo will get increasingly hungry until he starts to eat his own tail. If this happens, he will either start thrashing about from the pain or continue consuming his tail until there is nothing left. If either of these things happens, the world will fall into the great ocean and be destroyed.

Fortunately, the monkeys seem to have a very large supply of iron bars. But some traditions hold that the supply is being whittled down, and someday, none will be left.

HOPI PREDICTIONS OF THE END OF THE WORLD: THE NINE SIGNS

THE HOPI OF ARIZONA have one of the more detailed sets of predictions about what is to come during the run-up to the end of the world. These prophecies had been made before the arrival of European settlers, and some are rather disturbing, to say the least!

The Hopi believe that there are four ages to the world. The first was destroyed by fire, the second by ice, and the third by a great flood. We are now living in the fourth and final age, and the signs that it will soon end are all around us. Although there are different beliefs and traditions that the Native American peoples have not shared with outsiders, most agree that there are nine signs of the coming end:

1. Lighter-skinned invaders will arrive (the colonists traveling westward and settling on their lands).

2. There would be "spinning wheels" filled with voices (the settlers in their covered wagons gathering in long trains as they traveled west).

3. An unusual animal, like the bison but with different horns, would appear (the settlers brought large numbers of cattle with them).

4. The land will be visited by snakes of iron (a reference to trains?).

5. The land will be covered in a giant spider's web (this might refer to the railway network that was built to support train travel).

6. The land will become covered in "rivers of stone" (which seems to be our highway system).

7. The sea will turn black and many things will die when it does (maybe an oil spill?)

8. The young people of other lands and peoples would want to learn

about Hopi and native wisdom (there has certainly been a growing interest in the teachings of Native Americans and other indigenous peoples around the world).

9. The final sign is that people would live in the sky, but this home would eventually crash to Earth, looking like a blue star in the sky (possibly the International Space Station?).

After this last sign, the beginning of the end will commence. There will be war, destruction, misery, and death. Everyone will have to cooperate just to survive.

The eerie accuracy of these predictions gives some cause for concern. But know that the end of this fourth age might not be the final end. Most believe that after this time of terrible suffering, there will be a chance to enter a new, fifth age, where there will be peace and harmony among all things.

THE AZTECS AND THE FIVE SUNS

THE AZTEC EMPIRE WAS ONE of the great civilizations of the pre-Columbian Americas. Much of it was in what is now Mexico, and Mexico City is built on its old capital. Like many other Native American groups, the Aztecs believed in a series of ages that the world had been through. Unlike the Hopi, they believed that the four ages had already passed, and they were living in a fifth age. But this was no time of great peace and harmony; it was something far darker and stranger.

Each of the previous four ages had been created and destroyed when the gods battled. In each case, as the conflicts got worse, our world ended up being destroyed and then remade. But in this fifth age, the world is in a very different position. At the end of the fourth, the universe basically burned out. All was in darkness for fifty years, when the god Quetzalcoatl decided to go into Mictlan, the Aztec underworld, find some of the bones of the dead, and bring them back to life on Earth again. But this new world needed a sun, and there wasn't one. So a weak god named Nanahuatzin leaped into some flames and became a new sun. But he was not powerful like those that came before him, and couldn't shine bright enough. Other gods also sacrificed themselves to give this sun power, but it wasn't enough. The sun needed to be fed and renewed each day.

And that was where humanity could help out. As this fifth world was a cheap imitation of the ones that had come before it, and humans were basically just the dead brought back to life, they had to be willing to sacrifice themselves to the sun, just as the gods had. And so, the Aztecs developed religious rituals that involved cutting out the individuals' hearts and offering them up to the sun ... every day of the year!

By doing this, they could prevent this world from being destroyed by earthquakes. But they had to do it every day. If even one day went by without a human sacrifice, the world would begin to crumble, and what little is available in this shadowy and precariously constructed fifth world would also disappear into destruction and darkness. Thousands and thousands of people were killed every year in sacrifices (often these people were captured enemy warriors, criminals, and the like), all to keep the weak sun fueled for another day.

In the end, it wouldn't matter. Everyone knew that one day, the sacrifices would fail, or be forgotten, and then the world would start to collapse.

The Spanish colonists of the sixteenth century were shocked and horrified by what they saw, but in case we judge the Aztecs harshly, we need to remember that these colonists proceeded to murder the Aztecs by the thousands too, enslaved large numbers of them, destroyed their books and learning, and eliminated their civilization. What the Aztecs did was wrong, but what was done to them was equally wrong. And for them, the world really did end, not by earthquake, but by conquest.

OTHER AMERICAN FLOOD
AND FIRE MYTHS

THE TAINO PEOPLE of the Caribbean and Florida (who met Christopher Columbus on his first excursion to the New World) told a story about how there was once a young man who wanted to kill his father, but his father found out and banished him, and later killed him instead. The young man's father and mother kept their son's bones in a gourd. One day, they accidentally knocked over the gourd, and the son's bones turned into fish. Later, four brothers came by and saw the fish in the gourd while the man was away working in the fields. They ate the fish and then put the gourd back, but it fell to the ground and broke. All at once, water and more fish began to gush out of it, and soon the water covered the whole world.

The Quechua people of Peru have a tale about how a god came down to spend time celebrating with people at a party. No one recognized the god except for one young woman. The god was angry about the lack of recognition, and after instructing the young woman to climb a nearby mountain to be safe, he sent rains to flood and wash away the village, and apparently, the flood destroyed a lot of other land, as well.

In some traditions, a deluge is followed by a massive global fire, as if one disaster wasn't bad enough! Indigenous people in Venezuela have stories about a flood causing terrible destruction, but after that, the waters retreat and the sun dries everything out. In the Amazon and other areas, people have stories about how in the distant past, there was a time of evil and lawlessness. In response, the gods (or the world itself) sent a terrible punishment: clouds gathered and it rained blood! But soon, the blood turned to fire, killing everyone and destroying Earth. This story has been seen by some as a myth built off the actual eruption of a volcano; the "blood" could be lava, and the fire would be the hot, glowing rocks and ash that shot out before landing and setting the world aflame.

BELIEFS OF THE SIOUX AND CHEYENNE

TWO OF THE LARGER Native American groups of the American Plains have ideas about the end of the world that are a little less terrifying than those of the Aztecs, but no less fascinating. Like many cultures, both of these groups believe that the end is unavoidable, and we can only hope it will be put off for as long as possible. In both, an animal will determine our fate.

The White River Sioux say that the fate of the world depends on how an old black dog, named Shunka Sapa, behaves each day. He lives in a cave on the Great Plains, with an old woman. The cave is so hard to find that even these days, with more people and cars and highways, no one has ever stumbled upon it. The woman is so old that her face is said to look like a walnut.

She sits, as she has for more than a thousand years, knitting a strip for her robe using porcupine quills as needles. Beside her is a pot on a fire, which she also lit over a thousand years ago. In the pot, a berry soup called *wojapi* is boiling. Once in a while, the woman gets up to stir the pot before returning to her work. When her back is turned, the dog sneaks up and pulls out the piece of the strip she has been working on. This is a good thing, because the Sioux believe that if she ever finishes her work, the world will end at that very moment.

Unfortunately, Shunka Sapa has been undoing this work for so long that his own teeth have become worn down. One day, he will not be able to undo the woman's knitting.

The Cheyenne believe that somewhere out in the cosmos is a great pole, larger than we can conceive of any object being. This pole holds up the world and everything in it. But it won't last forever. Great White Grandfather Beaver is beside the pole, gnawing on it. He has been doing this for a very long time and is already about halfway through. When he is angry, he gnaws faster, and when he is calm, his progress through the wood slows.

When he finally gnaws all the way through, the pole will fall over and that will be the end of everything. The world will crash into a vast, bottomless nothingness, a fall no one will survive. Obviously, it was very important to the Cheyenne people not to make Great White Grandfather Beaver angry. They would never eat beaver flesh, or even touch the animal's skin. In keeping him calm, they knew that he would chew more slowly and the world would stick around a little bit longer.

THE LOST CITY OF ATLANTIS

THE STORY OF THIS AMAZING, doomed civilization has fascinated millions since the Greek philosopher Plato first wrote about it in the fourth century BCE. He seems to have meant the story to be instructive, a warning to people about the dangers of excessive pride, but it wasn't long before people began to believe that the city of Atlantis was real before it was destroyed in a terrible natural disaster.

Plato told about how this island's people were advanced and ruled over a vast land in the Atlantic Ocean thousands of years ago. But as they became more powerful, they also became increasingly cruel and evil. People from other nations started to resist, and in time, even the gods became incensed by the Atlanteans' behavior. So, they decided to destroy their civilization and sink the island with a series of earthquakes and floods. In just one day, the island disappeared, its people were killed, and the empire that had tried to dominate the world was destroyed.

A fascinating and terrifying story, but where had it come from? Many who study the story think that Plato just made the whole thing up, using it to stress the importance of behaving decently and not harming others, showing that even a mighty empire can fall if its people slip into evil. Others thought that Plato may have based his telling on historical records. Around the year 1600 BCE, there was a terrible volcanic

eruption on the island of Thera (now known as Santorini) in the Aegean Sea, off the east coast of Greece. This eruption destroyed a settlement called Akrotiri, a disaster that may have been remembered long enough to become part of people's myths.

Still others believe that Atlantis was a real place, an island or continent in the Atlantic Ocean that somehow sank beneath the waves. The problem is that looking at the floor of the Atlantic Ocean, we don't find any evidence for this. We can also see how, millions of years ago, South America would have fit together with Africa, before the continents drifted apart, so there would have been no room for a continent like Atlantis. But what if it were smaller, only a large island?

In recent decades, some have made a very bold and shocking claim: Atlantis is actually under the ice of Antarctica! They believe that the ice is recent, not millions of years old, and that the continent may have been farther north before geological changes "slid" it south. Pretty much no serious geologist or historian believes this theory, but it shows how the myth of Atlantis continues to fascinate people.

HENNY PENNY

THIS IS A POPULAR FOLKTALE from the British Isles and Ireland, and appears in many different versions. It's meant to make fun of the idea that someone can know when the world is coming to an end, and also the ridiculousness of fearing it.

In the Irish version, a hen named Henny Penny is standing under a hazelnut tree when a nut falls out of the tree and hits her on the tail. Even though she sees that it's only a nut, she foolishly believes that the sky must be falling. So she decides to go and warn her friends. She goes to see Cocky Locky, and then they go to Ducky Lucky, and then Goosey Poosey, and finally to the fox, Foxy Coxy. When they tell Foxy, he says that he will shelter each of them in a separate place to keep them safe when the end of the world happens. He does this, and each of them is hidden behind a different bush. And of course, the end never comes, and each realizes how foolish they were.

There are many versions of this story, and most have a violent ending. Henny Penny is convinced that the sky is falling and sets out to warn the king, picking up other birds along the way. The fox tricks each of the birds into coming into his home, one at a time, convincing them they will be safe there. As each bird goes in, he eats them, one after another. Obviously, the myth is urging people to think for themselves, and not jump to the worst possible conclusion.

Similar stories exist in Southern Asia. In one well-known version, rabbits in a forest hear a tree fall and think that the world must be ending, so they run along to tell the other animals, and eventually, all of them flee the forest. It is only when they meet with a lion, and he suggests that they go back to the source of the noise, that the animals realize their folly.

CHAPTER 2
SCIENCE

ALTHOUGH THERE ARE MANY RELIGIOUS AND MYTHIC visions of the end of the world, science has, over the course of the last few centuries, come up with many theories of its own.

When we say theory in science, we don't mean someone's guess. Instead, we're referring to individuals who have looked at all the known facts and used models to gain a better idea about what is likely to happen, and what is unlikely.

The stories in this section are all based on calculations and carefully examined ideas. That doesn't mean that they *will* happen, only that they *could*. Some are probably more likely than others. Many will never happen at all, at least not within the probable span of human existence. But some are uncomfortably close to happening, and will draw closer and closer if we let them …

From asteroid impacts to excessive pollution, from solar flares to deadly robots, from global pandemics to zombie apocalypses, here is a sampling of the ways we could meet our end, all based on real scientific ideas, which makes them that much more terrifying!

A HISTORY OF THE END OF THE WORLD

AN ASTEROID IMPACT

THERE'S NO DOUBT ABOUT IT: our planet being hit by a decent-sized asteroid would be a disaster, pretty much no matter where it struck. We've been lucky so far, but the truth is that space is surprisingly cluttered for being so vast, and countless objects have slammed into Earth in the past. In fact, if an asteroid hadn't wiped out the dinosaurs over sixty million years ago, there's a good chance that humans wouldn't be here, with an intelligent species of beings descended from dinosaurs evolving instead.

Asteroids are large sun-orbiting rocks whose orbits sometimes sometimes bring them into contact with planets. They've been shaping life on our world for as long as there's been life. And we've had some near misses in the recent past. The famous explosion over Tunguska, Siberia, in 1908, was probably an asteroid or comet that exploded in the air before it hit the surface. It's thought to have flattened eighty million trees over an area of more than 800 square miles. Obviously, it's very fortunate that the incident occurred in an unpopulated region. A few hours later, Earth would have turned a bit more, and it might have exploded over Europe or the United States.

Millions of space stones are out there in our solar system, especially in the asteroid belt, a region between Mars and Jupiter that may be the remains of a long-destroyed planet. Occasionally, some of the asteroids get thrown loose and start to orbit the sun in pathways that set them on collision courses with Earth and other planets.

Because we know that Earth and our moon have been bombarded by asteroids in the past, how likely is a similar event in the near future? The rather disconcerting answer: we have no idea. Even though various space agencies around the world monitor the night skies for asteroids, sometimes they fly disturbingly close by Earth and we see them just a few days before, or even a few days after!

If an asteroid of significant size—say, a mile wide—struck Earth, the damage would depend on where it hit. If the impact was on land, it would flatten everything for up to 200 miles in every direction, and kick up unimaginable amounts of dust and debris. That dust would spread into the atmosphere and blot out the sun, possibly for decades, which would kill a lot of the plants and animals that depend on them, including us. It's likely that only creatures that live in the deep sea would be spared.

If the same asteroid landed in the ocean, it would cause tidal waves hundreds of feet high to spread out in every direction, wiping out coastal cities and settlements, and pouring water inland for miles.

Now that you know what's at stake, you're probably wondering, What are the chances of one of these cataclysmic rocks slamming into us?

Unfortunately, they're kind of high. The most famous asteroid at the moment is Apophis (about 1,200 feet in width), which will have very close flybys to Earth in 2029, 2036, and 2068. Though collisions for its first two passes have been ruled out, there remains a small chance that it could strike the planet in 2068. And even though astronomers don't see any other asteroids out there big enough to cause worldwide devastation in the near future, there are always ones that we don't know about, and only find out about much later. Will we find out too late?

OUR EXPANDING SUN

OUR SUN IS A FAIRLY TYPICAL STAR in size and brightness, not so different from billions of others in the universe. And, like all stars, it goes through a life cycle. Ours is following a pretty predictable course right now, and most astronomers think that it will expand in size over billions of years. This will happen because the sun, at its core, fuses hydrogen into helium, a process known as nuclear fusion. As it does this, little by little, it is losing hydrogen, which causes it to heat up.

Over time, this heating up causes the rate of fusion and the size of the sun itself to increase. Eventually, scientists predict, our sun will become another type of star, known as a red giant. As it expands, it will eventually engulf and destroy Mercury, and probably also Venus— but what about Earth?

There are two theories about what might happen: One is that as the sun grows in size, it will lose mass, which means that Earth (and other, farther-away planets) might be thrown out of orbit and flung into space. Could Earth, Mars, and others become strange planets floating through the darkness of the universe, with no sun to orbit around?

The other theory is that Earth will remain in orbit of the sun when it becomes a red giant and will be burned up as it spirals into the star.

Neither of these options is very appealing, but one or the other is pretty much unavoidable. Our sun will eventually collapse into a dim star known as a white dwarf (most astronomers don't think it can become a black hole), around which maybe the gas planets (Jupiter, Saturn, etc.) will still orbit. In either case, Earth will be gone.

It's going to happen, and we can't do anything about it. The good news is that it won't happen for a very, very long time. The changes in the sun's energy might well mean that life on Earth will no longer be possible in about two billion years, anyway, and when our sun does begin to really grow, it will be in four or five billion years.

So, you can rest easy tonight, knowing that this cataclysm is a long way off!

SOLAR FLARES AND CORONAL MASS EJECTIONS

YOU MAY HAVE HEARD about how common solar flares and solar storms are. But what are they, exactly? Are they dangerous?

To begin, understand that our sun is a very active place. It's basically a gigantic nuclear reactor, always pulsing and churning as it fuses atoms in its core and sends massive amounts of energy into the solar system. Earth only absorbs a tiny amount of that energy, but it's enough to "power" life here, heating the planet, enabling photosynthesis, and making life on Earth, well, livable.

A solar flare is a burst of radiation from the sun that can last for anywhere from a few minutes to a few hours. A coronal mass ejection (or CME) is a burst of actual material from the sun, such as gas or plasma, that gets flung into space. In general, solar flares are no issue for us. Earth has a powerful magnetic field and atmosphere that protect it and us from radiation and its worst effects (though we all know what happens if we stay out in the sunlight too long).

The danger is if a powerful enough CME hits the planet at the right angle. If this happens, the CME can "slice open" the magnetic field for a short time (usually a few hours), allowing particles from the ejection to hit the North and South Poles. This might not seem like a big deal, but it can cause big trouble, threatening the communication systems and power grids we rely on.

We know that a massive storm called the Carrington Event hit our planet in 1859. At that time, our technology was not nearly as advanced, but the storm still managed to damage telegraph lines. As recently as 2003, a smaller storm caused power damage in places as far away from each other as the U.S. and Sweden.

What if we were hit again with a massive storm like the Carrington Event? Well, sorry to say, it could be really bad. Our power grids and electronics could be shut down for weeks, months, even years. It would take a massive amount of effort and money to get them up and running again, and in the meantime, society as we know it would basically end. Think about all of the things that rely on electricity: ATMs, credit card machines, gasoline pumps, heating, refrigeration, plumbing, nuclear power plants. There would be no way to treat our water, and it would become contaminated. Food would become harder and harder to find. The longer the blackout went on, the worse it would be. If it could be fixed in a few days or a week, things would get back to normal pretty quickly, but the longer it continued, the more dangerous and lawless things would get. Our whole way of life would be in jeopardy after only a few weeks.

What are the chances of this happening? We don't know for sure, but ejections like the 1859 event are not that uncommon, and have doubtless happened many times over the centuries. We wouldn't really have noticed them back then, because our civilization didn't run on electricity until the late nineteenth century. A big CME *will* happen again; it's just a matter of time, and we need to do more to be ready for it.

DARK MATTER AND EARTH IMPACTS

DARK MATTER IS ONE of the most mysterious things in the universe. No one's even sure if it *actually* exists. But it is used as an explanation for a big cosmic mystery: scientists noticed that galaxies rotated differently than they initially thought. The stars at the edges of a galaxy rotate faster than those closer to the center, and at the speeds they are moving, they should just go flying out into space. But they don't. Astronomers concluded that something invisible, but with mass, must be exerting its own force. There must be matter that we can't see, so-called "dark matter."

Many think that dark matter might make up more than 80 percent of all the matter in the universe, and that the things we can see (stars, galaxies, planets, ourselves) are just a small portion of what's out there.

One theory is that dark matter is made up of huge swarms of particles or atoms that don't react to light the way that "regular" matter does. These swarms may be floating through space, undetectable aside from the way they affect things around them. It's just a theory, as dark matter has not yet been proven to exist.

But what would happen if dark matter collided with Earth? Well, if it exists, it probably already has, and it probably doesn't do much at all.

One interesting theory says that some kinds of dark matter may indeed pose a danger to our planet. Some astronomers have theorized that a dense clump of dark matter sits along the plane of our galaxy, cutting it in half lengthwise. This means that as our solar system drifts around the Milky Way, sometimes we pass through this dark section.

As our solar system moves through the area of space with dark matter in it, that dark matter may have a gravitational effect on nearby asteroids and comets at the outer edges of the system, changing their orbits and send them hurtling toward Earth (see the previous section). Researchers have studied times in the past when there have been impacts on Earth, and they do line up pretty closely with the times when we would be drifting through this dark area. This alone doesn't prove that dark matter is causing asteroids to hit us, of course, but it is an interesting idea.

Is dark matter one of the causes of extinctions on Earth? We don't know yet, but let's hope we're not traveling through that area of space again soon, just in case!

A BLACK HOLE

BLACK HOLES ARE CURIOUS THINGS, things scientists still don't fully understand. The idea seems simple enough. All stars have life cycles. A star is born, grows, and eventually dies. One of the ways this death occurs is when the center of a very old star collapses in on itself. It explodes into what's called a supernova, sending pieces of itself out into space. Whatever remains can transform into something truly bizarre: a very dense bit of the dead star whose gravity is so strong that it starts to pull in everything around it, including light.

This gobbling up of light is why they are called black holes—as light cannot escape them, it is not possible to see what the inside of one looks like.

Obviously, black holes are very hard to detect, but astronomers believe they are common in most galaxies (there's a giant one at the center of our galaxy). Amazingly, a team was able to photograph one a few years ago, or rather, to photograph the light and material swirling around the hole as it is sucked in.

What happens to that matter? No one really knows. Some think that black holes might open doorways to other parts of the universe, or even other universes, but who wants to try to prove that theory?!

Fortunately for us, there are no black holes anywhere near Earth ... or are there? Stellar black holes (those that come from stars) are one kind of black hole, but scientists think other kinds likely formed during the big bang. Some of these black holes may be as small as a single atom, but would still have the mass of a mountain because they are so densely packed.

Could these tiny black holes be floating through space, causing damage to everything they come in contact with? Are they sucking up debris and rocks like miniature space vacuums? Maybe, but again, most astronomers don't seem to think they pose any real threat to us.

A HISTORY OF THE END OF THE WORLD

Still, what would happen if a small black hole, or a swarm of them, drifted by our planet? It would probably depend on the size, but if it were big enough, the planet, and everything on it, would start to be dragged toward the black hole, in a process known as "spaghettification." You, the planet, and everything would start to be stretched as the gravity of the black hole pulled us in, turned us into long, spaghettilike strands by the tremendous forces acting upon our bodies.

The worst thing is, we'd probably never see it coming. Some astronomers might detect unusual signs of gravity in our vicinity, but what could we do if a small black hole flew on by and decided to take a bite out of us? Not much, sorry to say! So, although it's very unlikely, if you wake up one morning and start feeling like you're being pulled up into the air, and your body starts getting longer and thinner, you'll know it isn't a dream ...

VACUUM DECAY

NO, THIS HAS NOTHING TO DO with the machine you use to clean floors breaking down. It's actually one of the more frightening concepts about the potential end of the universe, a rather complex theory that says a universe, at a fundamental level, can be in one of two states: a true vacuum, which is a very stable state where very little happens, and a false vacuum, also known as a "metastable" universe. Recent studies of subatomic particles have suggested that our universe is a false vacuum.

These kinds of universes are less stable than those in a true vacuum, and an event with enough energy could cause a very big problem. This issue could occur at the subatomic level—with a large enough disturbance causing a tiny portion of the false vacuum to turn into a true vacuum. Such a transformation would be bad, very bad. This bubble of true-vacuum universe would begin to expand very rapidly, at the speed of light, and as it did, would destroy everything in its path—as in completely wipe it out. Because it is traveling at the speed of light, we might never see it coming, and even if we did, there would be nothing we could do.

One of the more terrifying thoughts is that this might have already happened, somewhere way out in the universe, and the bubble is expanding, destroying everything as it grows. Of course, the universe being as big as it is, it would still take billions of years for the bubble to expand far enough to wipe out all the stars and galaxies, but it could be out there somewhere, hurtling toward us. Because the light of distant galaxies is only reaching us now, those galaxies could have been destroyed millions of years ago, and we just don't know it.

There is an area of space called the Boötes void that mysteriously has almost no galaxies at all. Its center is more than 700 million light-years away, and no one knows for sure why this area of space is so empty. Is an expanding true vacuum bubble out there, wiping out galaxies as it grows? It's a scary thought, though believed not to be likely. Most scientists think the chance a true vacuum could actually expand in our universe is very, very low. Some have suggested that, even if it could, it wouldn't happen for several billion years.

A GAMMA-RAY BURST

GAMMA-RAY BURSTS (GRBs) are the most intense of all astronomical events, far brighter than supernovas, and far more violent. They can happen when two neutron stars collide and form a black hole, when a black hole swallows a neutron star, or when a star explodes in a supernova. They are short, lasting anywhere from a few seconds to a few hours. You can't see them with the naked eye because they occur outside the visible spectrum of light, but the effects on our planet would be devastating if we found ourselves in the path of the energy created by the burst.

Just *how* devastating would depend on how far away the blast took place. If the burst was several thousand light-years away and happened today, the rays would not reach Earth for those thousands of years. If it already had happened thousands of years ago, and showed up here tomorrow, the effects might be not much more than knocking out satellites and causing power, internet, and communication disruptions. Much of the burst would have dissipated over that long journey and our atmosphere and magnetic field would probably protect us. It might cause a slight increase in radiation levels and dim the sun's light a bit, though only for a few years.

But if a burst happened a bit closer, say, "only" a few hundred light-years away, we could be in a lot more trouble. The radiation from the burst would destroy our ozone layer, making us vulnerable to all kinds of space radiation, including the radiation that emanates from our own sun. Plant species would begin to die off rapidly, and all of the creatures that eat them would also be in danger. Without those plants, the oxygen in our atmosphere would begin to drop until it reached a point where living things literally would not be able to breathe the air around them.

If a burst happened anywhere closer to our planet than this, we'd be toast. It would likely strip away our atmosphere, killing most life suddenly. The ensuing radiation would finish off anything that remained.

So, what are the odds of a terrible thing like this happening? Well, so far, no gamma-ray bursts have been detected in our own galaxy, which is good news, because it means the ones we've found are much farther away and might shoot off in an entirely different direction. But a gamma-ray burst of some sort might have been the cause of a mass extinction event on Earth 450 million years ago. Obviously, it was not enough to wipe out all life or destroy the atmosphere, but it seems to have been close enough to be devastating. If we've already been hit once, it means that we might be hit again. Some scientists think this won't be likely for millions of years, but you never know ...

A STRAY EXOPLANET

THOUGH THIS END-OF-THE-WORLD SCENARIO seems like something out of a science fiction movie, it is something that, along with asteroids and comets, astronomers at least have to consider when they examine the dangers lurking in space.

Probably countless planets are drifting through space that were once a part of their own solar systems, but for whatever reason, they were bumped out of orbit and are now adrift in space as they sail through the endless dark of the vast universe.

And they could be a problem for us. In the search for planets outside of our solar system, we have been able to detect several thousand of them by observing the stars they orbit around. The planets themselves are too far away to see on their own, so scientists have to look for evidence of movement in front of these stars. Once they determine that something is there, they can begin to calculate the planet's size and type, how far away it is from its star, and much more. But we can't really see the planets themselves.

If we can only see planets because of their suns, what does that mean for stray planets floating in darkness? That's right. We can't really see them, or even know if they are there. And there's the problem: what if a big exoplanet hidden in the endless dark of space is hurtling toward us and we don't even know it's coming, and won't until it's too late?

It's not impossible, but it's important to remember that space is unimaginably vast. Really, try looking at a scale map of the solar system online—you'll be blown away by just how large our relatively little solar system is. Two tiny objects like planets are very unlikely to come into each other's paths, certainly not close enough to hit each other. But that's not to say it couldn't happen, or hasn't happened in the past.

It's now believed that a planet about twice the size of Earth smashed into Uranus billions of years ago, essentially knocking it on its side. Also, our moon was probably created during the early period of our solar system, when the young Earth was hit by a planet about the size of Mars. Debris created by this collision eventually became the moon.

The difference in these cases was that these planets were already orbiting our sun; they didn't come from outside the solar system. So, although a deadly exoplanet could be out there, we're far more likely to be hit by an asteroid. Which probably doesn't make you feel any better!

A SUPERVOLCANO

NO, THIS ISN'T A SUPERHERO VOLCANO! It's something a lot less heroic, and a lot more deadly. And if one were to erupt in the modern world, it might just be the end for all of us. A supervolcano is defined by having the largest value on the splendidly named "Volcanic Explosivity Index." These volcanoes are especially powerful, able to expel ash and magma amazing distances.

Supervolcanoes aren't like the mountains you might be used to seeing: a cone shape with ash and lava spewing out of the top. They occur when magma (lava) in Earth's mantle rises underneath the crust and doesn't have anywhere to go, causing pressure to build up. Fortunately, this can take a very long time to happen. Unfortunately, when it does happen, the results can be absolutely catastrophic, with unimaginable amounts of energy released, destructive lava spilling out, and ash being spread for thousands of miles.

It might disturb you to know that supervolcanoes are found in various places around the world; there are several in the western United States, a cluster in South America between Chile and Argentina, a few in southern Japan, one in New Zealand, and several in Indonesia. There is a smattering of them in other places, too, so nowhere is really safe!

One such supervolcano that geologists and others are keeping a close (and sometimes anxious) eye on is the Yellowstone caldera, in Wyoming's Yellowstone National Park. As you probably know, this area is famous for its hot water geysers, like Old Faithful, and these are created by the same volcanic processes that are slowly allowing magma to build up under the site. In fact, this area has had three known super-eruptions in its recent geologic history, one at just over two million years ago, one at about 1.3 million years, and the most recent at about 664,000 years ago. And although there is no proof that another eruption will happen soon, we can't rule out the possibility.

What would happen if the Yellowstone caldera had a full-on supervolcanic eruption? The area within about 350 miles would be

covered in at least three feet of deadly, hot ash that would kill most of the life present and destroy countless buildings, roads, and so on. The farther one got from the eruption, the less deep the ash would be, but it could reach as far as San Francisco in the West and Chicago in the East, causing unthinkable carnage. The atmosphere would be blanketed in lighter ash that floated miles above the ground. This could block out the sun and create unnatural winter-like conditions that might last for five to ten years. This lack of sun would make it impossible for plants to grow, so mass starvation would likely set in at some point.

The good news is that some geologists think that the Yellowstone caldera will never erupt again, or at least not at the level of a supervolcano. But don't get cocky. A supervolcano erupts on average about every 100,000 years on Earth, and could happen anywhere in the world.

INTENSE HEAT/CO$_2$

GLOBAL WARMING IS A PHRASE we've been hearing for decades. The idea is that too much of the carbon dioxide our industries and cars give off is entering the atmosphere, more than plants can remove. As a result, it just hangs there. Carbon dioxide is a major greenhouse gas, which means that it allows heat to enter an area and then prevents it from escaping.

Think of getting into a car on a hot summer day. It's hot outside, but when you get in, it's blazing, sometimes so much so that you burn yourself on the seat! That's the greenhouse effect, and that's what the extra carbon dioxide in our atmosphere is slowly doing to Earth. Buildups of greenhouse gases have occurred naturally at many points in the past—for example, Earth during the time of the dinosaurs was warmer than it is today.

But the situation we are currently facing is one of our own making. Scientists are able to measure levels of carbon dioxide in the atmosphere going back hundreds of thousands of years by looking at plant life and ice that can trap it. For at least the last 800,000 years, carbon dioxide levels have been pretty stable, and never above a few spikes of 300 parts per million.

Looking at recent decades, we can see that the levels of the gas have risen quite a lot, from around 280 in 1950 to over 400 now. This is due almost entirely to our machines, car emissions, intense factory farms, livestock, and other industries that use a lot of energy.

The average surface temperature on Earth has gone up by about 2 degrees Fahrenheit (just over 1 degree celsius) since the end of the nineteenth century, and much of that rise has happened in the last forty years or so. The six warmest years ever recorded on Earth have all happened since 2014.

So what happens because of this warming? The oceans begin to trap energy, raising their temperatures and making them more acidic. This

A HISTORY OF THE END OF THE WORLD

can affect marine life and kill off sensitive species, coral, and so on. The ice at the North and South Poles has begun to melt, and this has led to rising sea levels. We're already seeing more coastal flooding around the world. There can be more extreme storms, because hotter air is colliding with cooler air in increasingly violent ways. Larger and stronger hurricanes are one effect of these heightened exchanges. Dry areas are more likely to have droughts, leading to crops failing, and people and animals suffering. Drier areas of land also have larger forest fires.

Some skeptics have tried to say that this is all a natural process that Earth goes through, shifting between hotter and colder periods, but most scientists now reject this idea. And even if it were true, it still means that we have to pay attention to what is happening and fix things where we can.

Remember, the planet Venus probably once had a surface not unlike Earth's. But with increasing amounts of greenhouse gases filling the atmosphere over time, its surface temperature is now about 900 degrees Fahrenheit!

A NEW ICE AGE

WE OFTEN HEAR ABOUT GLOBAL WARMING and how the planet will continue to get hotter over time, causing widespread damage. But what about the other possibility? What if Earth were to cool off and plunge into another ice age? This is not as impossible as it might seem at first.

Ice ages come and go depending on several factors: changes to Earth's temperature, levels of greenhouse gases, the position of the continents, changes in Earth's orbit around the sun, and even shifts in the oceans' currents. Any or all of these things can change the overall temperature of the planet, making it hotter or cooler. When an ice age happens, water gets trapped at the poles. The levels of the oceans go down (because so much water is trapped in ice), and massive glaciers carve their way across the land, destroying everything in their path. There were once massive sheets of ice across northern Europe, for example, and we can still see how that ice carved its way through rock, making huge valleys between mountain peaks.

The periods of ice can last for tens of thousands of years, advancing and retreating at differing rates. It isn't that suddenly everything is covered in ice and then it's gone just as abruptly. It's a slow and gradual process, for the most part.

We are now living in what is called an "interglacial" period. In other words, we are between ice ages. We've been in this warmer pattern for more than 11,000 years now, and according to some predictions, this will continue for at least 28,000 years before the ice begins to advance again. Due to current issues with global warming, some think that this new ice age is getting pushed even farther out, commencing in 50,000 years or more. But one thing is certain: a new ice age will come again, whether or not we want it to.

Is it something that we need to be concerned about? The general belief is that ice ages take a very long time to develop and grow, so we're not in any danger of seeing something so dramatic and terrible in our lives. But some researchers fear that smaller ice ages might come before then. The period between about 1300 and 1850 is often known as the "Little Ice Age," when temperatures in the Northern Hemisphere were cooler and winters were more severe. So, even though we are in a warming period, cooler eras lasting for centuries can still happen.

The present warming could even lead to cooling. If temperatures get hot enough in the Atlantic Ocean to melt all the ice on Greenland (a process currently under way), all that cold and fresh water pouring into the ocean might be enough to disrupt the flow of the Gulf Stream, an air current that brings warmer air up from the Gulf of Mexico and deposits it in Europe. If that flow is cut off, Europe and the Northern Hemisphere could get much colder, and very quickly.

Could another baby ice age strike, one that would be strong enough to damage our civilization and cause widespread death and suffering? We don't know, but it is something to keep an eye on.

––––––––––

MAGNETIC FIELD FAILURE

EARTH IS SPECIAL, in that it is protected by a powerful magnetic field, which is generated within the planet. The outer core of the planet is made up of mostly molten iron and nickel, and as they churn, they basically turn our world into a giant magnet. This force is important for life on the planet, because the magnetic field flows out into space (some say it's like invisible strands of spaghetti) and interacts with the solar wind, helping to shield our planet from the damaging effects of solar ultraviolet radiation.

What would happen if this field failed, or started to? We might not notice at first, but over time, there would be an increase in the incidence of cancers and other health problems. One of the major problems we would notice quickly is disruptions to our satellite technology, which would affect not only the satellites themselves, but also everything that depends on them, such as computers, cell phones, the internet, and so on, power grids would also be at risk.

The field itself probably won't fail any time soon (some scientists think it will take billions of years for this to happen), but there is some concern that it is getting weaker, which carries its own problems. One issue is that the magnetic poles of the world flip from time to time. This means that north becomes south and south becomes north. Now, this doesn't mean that the planet itself will flip upside down, because there is no "up" or "down" in space. But if there is a pole shift, our equipment will get messed up. Compasses would no longer work, for example, and migrating birds that rely on the magnetic field for guidance would be confused about where to go.

A pole reversal would weaken the magnetic field, but probably not get rid of it completely. Still, this could continue to cause problems for a very long time. A weaker magnetic field might allow for some damage to the ozone layer, for example, because more of the damaging rays from the sun would be getting through.

Are the poles about to shift? We're not sure, but the weakening of the field over the last 150 years or so suggests that it might. Many books about pole shifts have been written, some that tie the phenomenon to the apocalypse. But the truth is, it seems to be a fairly normal part of the magnetic field's process to go back and forth between stronger and weaker periods, and we might just be in a weaker period right now.

BEE DIE-OFF

WE'VE ALL SEEN BEES busily at work on flowers in springtime, going from plant to plant, their little bee legs sticky with pollen, which they will transfer to other plants as they continue on their way. Bees—and other pollinators like butterflies, moths, and flies—all play a crucial role in helping many plants reproduce. A lot of the fruit trees and other plants would not be able to make more of themselves and produce fruit without nature's little helpers.

That's one of the big problems we're facing right now. Large die-offs of bee populations are becoming more common of late. There have been many theories about why this is happening, but it seems to be a combination of several things: overuse of pesticides, diseases, parasites (other little bugs and organisms), and loss of natural habitat. What this means is that no one, easy solution will fix the problem. But it's a problem that scientists realize we have to fix, and soon.

One of the worst pesticides is a group known as neonicotinoids, which are used in many crops that honeybees rely on. These pesticides have been found to cause problems with bee memory and navigation, meaning they can literally get lost and forget where their hives are. When this happens, they fly away somewhere else and die.

This is all depressing, but is there a bigger problem? Yes. You see, farmers, even the big agricultural companies, rely on pollinators to ensure their crops continue to flower and remain productive. If there aren't enough bees (or no bees at all) to do the job, we're really in trouble. We don't have good artificial ways to pollinate, and if the bees aren't there to do the work for us, we won't have enough food. It really is as simple as that.

Some studies have even suggested that if the bees died out completely, humanity would have only four more years to live before mass starvation set in. There simply wouldn't be a way to produce enough food for everyone, and civilization as we know it would soon come to an end. Small bands of humans might be able to go back to hunting, but if there were no bees, food supplies would be very scarce.

There is some good news—some bee colonies seem to be making a comeback in recent years, but the situation changes from year to year, so it's too soon to predict that the crisis is over, or whether it's only a slight upturn before another big downturn. It's essential that we continue to monitor the health of bees and other pollinators and find ways to eliminate the damaging pesticides that are harming them. We also need to look for ways to prevent infections, and work to make sure that bee habitats don't get destroyed. Our lives depend on it!

POLLUTION

POLLUTION HAS BEEN A SERIOUS concern around the world for more than a century, and though there have been many good efforts to combat it, it continues to get worse in some places. Pollution can come from many sources: smog in the air from cars and industry, toxic chemicals dumped into oceans and freshwater supplies, excessive use of pesticides on crops, groundwater contaminated by poisons, and more. These polluted environments usually end up causing damage to plants, animals, and humans, and frequently on uncomfortably large scales.

Pollution is a side effect of our industrial civilizations: we drive cars that push exhaust into the air. We use plastic items made with chemicals that end up in the atmosphere or water. We use large amounts of pesticides to protect crops on large farms. We lock our garbage away in massive landfills that continue to expand; from there, numerous toxic chemicals can seep into the ground and cause problems elsewhere.

There's no one easy "pollution solution," because it issues from so many sources. But it's obvious that more needs to be done to clean up polluted environments. It's not just about preserving the land for the future (though that's a worthy goal). Polluted environments can cause problems all along the food chain. A chemical spill in a river or ocean may make fish unsafe to eat. If a spill occurs in an area that depends on commercial fishing to support the local economy, the people who do the fishing work might soon be out of jobs, because they can't safely sell what they catch. Oil spills can cause the same kind of problems in the ocean. Or maybe people eat fish before it's known that they are contaminated, and end up getting very sick.

Many cities around the world continue to grow to absolutely huge sizes, often 20 million or more people. Their governments now have to limit the numbers of cars that can be in the cities, and even which days people can drive. The skies in some cities of the world are constantly hazy, even yellow or orange, because there is so much exhaust in the air. All of this takes a terrible toll on human health, and the air is so bad at times that people have to stay inside or go out wearing masks.

There are vast masses of plastics floating in the oceans, creating desolate areas where sea life can't live. If too much of the food chain in the ocean is disrupted, it will have a knock-on effect for life on land as well.

Could the world come to an end because of too much pollution? Probably not abruptly, but over time, environments could be degraded so badly that they would make large areas around the world uninhabitable. Many scientists and researchers think we may be only thirty or forty years away from this happening, unless we act now.

ECOLOGICAL COLLAPSE

WE'VE BEEN HEARING stories about damage to the environment for more than a half century, and although many people genuinely care about saving the world, it does seem like the damage keeps happening, even though so many are trying to help.

There have been five major extinctions during the history of living things, and although some of them were terrible, life always found a way to rebound. But just because some life might find a way to make it through the next large extinction doesn't mean that we will. What are some of the bigger concerns that humans face? Here are just a few:

The ozone layer: Scientists discovered in the 1970s that certain chemicals used by industries were damaging the ozone layer. This is a portion of the atmosphere that helps filter out harmful ultraviolet rays from the sun. Fortunately, the world's governments came together in the late 1980s and agreed to phase out these chemicals, which has resulted in the ozone recovering. But work still needs to be done to make sure that it stays safe.

Oceans: Pollution, toxic dumping, plastic waste, and overfishing are just some of the problems the world's oceans are facing. Any of these can combine to kill species and upset the delicate ecological balance. The big fear is that if enough smaller life-forms are damaged or die off, it will adversely affect the entire food chain, with terrible effects on larger life-forms such as fish and whales.

Amphibians: Amphibians such as frogs and salamanders are sometimes called indicator species, meaning that if researchers start to see them dying off in large numbers, it usually means that the entire ecosystem they live in is in danger, because they live part of their lives on land and part in water. Amphibians can be affected by pollution, invasive new species, destruction of their habitats, climate change, and a number of other threats. Scientists monitor the health of amphibian species closely, because that can help them determine if there is greater damage in an area than it seems at first glance.

Soil erosion: Land that is irresponsibly farmed can become barren. Unfortunately, this reckless husbandry is happening more and more often with the rise of big agricultural farms that try to keep squeezing as much as they can out of the huge plots of land they have. Traditionally, famers would allow one of their fields to lie fallow, or unused, for a season or two, allowing it to rest and regenerate. If this practice is not followed, the soil becomes depleted of nutrients and loses the ability to grow anything. If this happens over too large an area, it will become much harder to feed all of the planet's inhabitants.

Deforestation: Earth continues to lose trees at an alarming rate, and not just in the rainforests. Trees are literally the "lungs of the world," putting oxygen back into the atmosphere as they remove carbon dioxide. Cutting down large amounts of forest for cattle ranching and farming will make it literally harder to breathe in the future.

PANDEMICS

PANDEMICS HAVE BEEN with humanity throughout our history. In 2020 and 2021, we all experienced a pandemic, something many thought would not happen in our lifetimes. COVID-19 is a dangerous virus, a reality that should not be denied. Fortunately, it is not as deadly as it could have been. The idea of a tiny, invisible virus sweeping the world and killing or harming millions of people is a scary one, and many thrillers have been based around such an event.

Unfortunately, viruses are all around us, and they are always mutating. We never know from year to year what might happen, what might emerge. This is why we are encouraged to get a flu shot every year— different variants of the virus arise, and vaccine developers have to make an educated guess about which strains are most likely to be floating around. This is also why, even if you get the shot, you might still get sick if you encounter a variant you haven't been vaccinated for.

What happens if a virus mutates into something really dangerous? We have a pretty good idea based on what happened during the flu pandemic of 1918 to 1920. Researchers estimate that about one-third of the world's population (500 million) became infected with the virus, and at least 50 million died. That's about 10 percent of everyone who was infected. It swept over the world and spared no one, rich or poor. It was very contagious and very deadly, so virulent that it actually affected the young and healthy in equal measure to the elderly and feeble.

That serves as a warning, a reminder that these things are beyond our control, just as we've seen with COVID-19. We've had to wear masks, shelter at home, and try to avoid people as much as possible while vaccines were being developed. And we're lucky that scientists have been researching these kinds of viruses for a long time, which made it easier to create the vaccines rapidly.

But what would happen if something brand new showed up that we didn't understand so well? Or what if a super-deadly virus like Ebola (which makes people hemorrhage internally) mutated into a version that was more transmittable, and maybe lived in the body for longer, allowing it to be carried across the globe? Well, we'd be in real trouble, even with all of our scientific knowledge. With global airline travel and mass gatherings of people every day, a disease like this could possibly kill a billion people or more, a loss that is hard to even fathom. Nowhere in the world would be safe from it.

How likely is this to happen? Unfortunately, we don't know. But, as the recent pandemic has shown, it *will* happen again.

MUTATED BACTERIA

BACTERIA ARE EVERYWHERE, covering everything on Earth. It's said that we have more bacteria in our bodies than human cells ... so what does that make us, really? Well, this isn't the place for such philosophical discussions, so let's leave that one alone for the moment.

The staggering number of bacteria means that not only are they everywhere, they are also essential for life on Earth to exist. And that's fine. Every day we come into contact with bacteria that are either completely harmless to us, or at least don't do any damage. But what about the ones that do cause harm?

There are plenty of those out there, and though most don't present too much danger, there are some really nasty ones, waiting to jump into our bodies and eat us alive! Sort of. Just what can they do? Well, you've probably heard of the "Black Death" that spread across medieval Europe, beginning in the 1340s. That was also known as bubonic plague, and was caused by tiny bacteria called *Yersinia pestis*. The bacteria infected fleas, which lived on rats. The rats would travel to other locations by ship, and once there, they would scurry away from the ship and into the city. The fleas would jump off at random, looking for their next meal.

That meal just happened to be people. Fleas would jump onto them and bite them, drinking their blood (ew!) and infecting them with the plague. What would happen to those infected? Well at some point after infection, the person might get a fever and chills, a headache and muscle aches. But the most common sign was the swelling of lymph nodes on the neck and groin, forming large bumps called "buboes." After that, things would get grim very fast, and the person would get very sick and almost always die. This Black Death spread through western Europe from 1347 to 1353, and is believed to have killed at least one-third of the population.

The good news is that antibiotics can easily treat plague these days. The bad news is that more and more bacteria are becoming resistant to antibiotics as they evolve. So what happens if an infection like the plague becomes immune to antibiotics? We're in a lot of trouble. Oh, and there's another version of the plague called pneumonic plague, which is spread by coughing and sneezing. What if that mutates to become immune to treatment?

And other really nasty bacteria out there are proving to be very hard to cure with antibiotics. It's an issue of great concern to many doctors and health associations, and the race is on to find new forms of antibiotics that can deal with these bacteria, and some researchers are even trying to manufacture viruses that can eat them. But this will always be a struggle, because bacteria will always adapt and change to survive.

We've been lucky for the last fifty years or so, but our time as masters of bacteria may be coming to an end, and if a very strong and dangerous version of something emerges and we can't treat it, it might wipe out much of the population with relative swiftness.

INTERPLANETARY CONTAMINATION

WE DRIFT THOUGH the vastness of space, orbit around our sun, happily protected by our atmosphere, magnetic field, ozone layer, and a number of other things that keep life on Earth spinning along. But what might happen if something from outside of our world collided with us?

Many scientists have wondered if life on Earth began someplace else in the universe. Were the building blocks of life already present, or were they carried here, hitching a ride on a meteor that slammed into the planet back in the early days of its existence? It's an intriguing thought, and if true, it means that we are all extraterrestrials of a sort! We know that some rocks ejected from Mars found their way to Earth. One such rock was discovered in 1996, and showed signs of fossilized bacteria, meaning that life could have come from Mars! This made headlines at the time, but later, most scientists rejected the idea (for a number

of reasons that are too technical to get into here). Still, the idea that microscopic life could be elsewhere in the universe is one that most scientists take seriously.

We know that here on Earth, tiny organisms can survive in extreme environments, so there's no reason why such life-forms couldn't survive on Mars or moons like Titan and Europa. Microscopic life may well be common in the universe, happily living on planets and moons that no higher life-forms could ever exist on.

This could be a big problem for us. If bacteria and/or viruses live on other worlds, what would happen if one of them hitched a ride on an asteroid or meteorite that crashed into our planet? What might happen if we came into contact with an infectious extraterrestrial bacteria or space virus?

Well first, we would have no natural immunity, because it would never have been on this world before. That might not be a problem if it were harmless, but what if it was aggressive and dangerous? It might create strange new symptoms we'd never seen before, and as we tried to identify it by comparing it to our known diseases, we'd come up short. Would we ever even know that it was from outer space? Maybe only if it resulted in symptoms so bizarre that we could be sure no pathogen on Earth could cause that. And then we would have to scramble to try to contain it. Would it only affect humans, or animals, too? What about plant life? What if it could potentially wipe out all forms of life on Earth? A famous book and movie, *The Andromeda Strain*, uses this conceit as its backbone (see page 196).

Fortunately, the chances of something like this happening are not too likely—at least we don't think! But small objects collide with Earth all the time. Even if they are not large enough to cause much damage on their own, they could be transporting some very unwelcome visitors!

A ZOMBIE APOCALYPSE

ZOMBIES! THE LIVING DEAD! Those that have returned from the grave and now shamble across the world, eager to eat someone. One bite, and you'll become a zombie yourself. The idea of masses of people turned into mindless walking things is creepy, especially if only a few humans survive to try to fight them off.

Zombies have been the subject of some very scary (and frequently gross) movies and TV shows over the years, and for many, they are gripping entertainment. But it's all just fantastic fiction, isn't it? There's no real science behind it, right? Well...

Parasites: Some parasites in nature, mostly in the animal kingdom, can get into the brain and change behavior. One example, *Toxoplasmosa*, attacks the brain of rats and makes them run toward cats, who then eat them. This allows the parasite to grow in the cat, until pooping it out. Then, it finds another rat to infect. It's been estimated that large numbers of humans have this parasite in them as well; it just doesn't

affect us. But what if it did? What if a mutated form started making us behave more violently, and suddenly millions of people were storming around like crazed zombies? Some forms of fungus attack insects and do the same thing. What if one of these mutated and got into a group of humans, or we all breathed in its spores? Could half the people in the world be turned into zombielike creatures in only a few weeks?

Disease mutations: Viruses like rabies and even severe forms of the flu can attack the brain and cause damage to the frontal lobe. When this happens, the person can become closed off to the outside world and react very violently when anyone tries to talk to them, touch them, and so on. They might not move, or they might wander around slowly, their mind blank but ready to act out when something comes along, just like a zombie would. If a pandemic of one of these viruses hit humanity, it could turn most of us into mindless beings that attack one another at the drop of a hat.

Haitian zombies: The original stories of zombies come from the island of Haiti, where some people long ago developed a way of using a dangerous toxin to make it seem like someone had died, only to bring them out of it later and put them to work on farms and in other places as mind-numbed slaves. But this kind of zomblie would need to get a dose of this toxin on a regular basis, or the effects would wear off. But what if this could be weaponized? Maybe put into a water supply? Would the whole population soon become shambling zombies under someone's control?

Regenerating dead tissue: There has been a lot of research in recent decades on how to revive dead tissues, especially brain cells. You can see where this is going. What if a scientist or group with evil intentions decided to try to regenerate the brains of dead patients, but could only bring them back to do the most basic functions: walk, stumble around, growl, and so on. You'd have real-life, completely terrifying zombies! This may seem like science fiction, but work is already under way in several labs around the world to try to repair damaged brain cells in the hopes of curing various diseases and health problems. Let's just hope this doesn't get out of hand!

NUCLEAR WAR

ONE OF THE BIG FEARS since the beginning of the nuclear arms race in the 1950s has been global nuclear war: a hasty exchange of devastating nuclear weapons that would wipe out most life on Earth. During the 1950s and 1960s especially, the United States and the Soviet Union were poised with hundreds of nuclear missiles pointed at each other, a show of force that was viewed as necessary to ensure that neither side would ever use them. The idea of "mutually assured destruction" was enough to keep anyone from being so crazy as to try to launch a strike in a war that both sides knew could not be won.

At various times, both sides would meet and sign new treaties to reduce the number of weapons, or to make sure that they wouldn't be launched, and the world could keep turning.

The problem was, over those years, other countries began developing and acquiring these weapons, too. They would claim it was for their own protection. Today, for example, India and Pakistan both have nuclear weapons, and they are pointed at each other, because the countries have been rivals for many decades. North Korea also has some missiles. Exactly how many and how powerful they are is not known, but because the country is closed to the world and likes pretty much no one, it's a development to keep an eye on.

People already have an uncomfortable knowledge of what the result of a massive nuclear exchange would be. Countless movies, TV shows, and books have told the story of what life might be like in a world that has been exposed to terrible amounts of radiation. Even a limited war (say, between two smaller nations) would still cause terrible devastation, and radioactive materials might well drift all over the world, carried on the wind.

A big enough war would not only destroy most big population centers, but likely plunge the world into a "nuclear winter" that continued for years, with all the debris and ash thrown up into the atmosphere blocking out sunlight. This in turn would kill off many of the plants

A HISTORY OF THE END OF THE WORLD

and animals not destroyed in the initial explosions. And, of course, upward of billions of people could die in a single day. It would be the most horrific event in the history of Earth, even worse than the asteroid impacts of the past. Even if life did manage to survive, it would be changed forever.

Many organizations are working to prevent something so terrible from ever becoming a reality, and more and more governments are agreeing that stronger controls on nuclear weapons must be in place. There are bans on testing and limits on numbers of missiles, but many feel that we need to do more. Considering what would happen if one country crossed the line, it's hard not to agree.

BIOLOGICAL WARFARE

WAR HAS ALWAYS BEEN WITH US, and unfortunately, we seem to keep coming up with new, increasingly horrible ways to kill each other. One of the more terrifying is the concept of biological warfare. This is the deliberate creation of dangerous viruses and bacteria in labs, which can then be attached to weapons and used against enemy soldiers or the population of an enemy country. Yes, it's absolutely horrible and evil, and yes, it's banned by international law. But that doesn't mean that there aren't some who continue to work on these terrible projects in secret.

There are many different forms, and the viruses, bacteria, and so on, can be lethal or not, depending on what the objective is. One example might be to target an army with a strong form of the flu virus, to make them so sick that they can't fight. Or, it might be launching some plant disease at a nation's crops, with the intention of wiping them out and pushing the population to the brink of starvation. The same thing could also be done to their farm animals. The enemy country would have no choice but to surrender and hope for aid from other countries.

Most countries do not work on these projects. But some do, and as you can imagine, they don't tell anyone they're doing it. In these cases, another large threat is what would happen if some of this material was stolen. Could a rogue nation or terrorist group use bioweapons to blackmail the world? It's a big concern, and one that is taken seriously.

Another concern is about what might be created in a lab itself. What if, for example, scientists in one country create a very dangerous form of the flu, and for some reason, it's either stolen or accidentally released into the world? This is what happens in the opening of horror writer Stephen King's novel, *The Stand* (see page 192). A very dangerous flu virus created for the military gets out of a lab, and ends up infecting and killing most of the people in the world over the next month.

Could something like this really happen? It's not likely, but we can't say that it's impossible—there are theories suggesting that COVID-19 was originally a biological weapon that was accidentally (or maybe deliberately) released into the world.

TERRORISM GONE AMOK

TERRORISM AND TERRORIST attacks are not a recent thing. They've been with us for a very long time, and only the technology has changed. The English word *assassin*, for example, comes from the name of a mysterious group that lived high in the mountains of Syria in the twelfth century and terrorized the local populations, including the king.

So, groups attempting to use threats and violence to get what they want are not new. But these days, the options they have to carry out their threats can be exceptionally dangerous. Governments around the world have developed all kinds of weapons—nuclear, chemical, and biological—to be used in times of war. Although many of these are now illegal under agreements signed by these nations, they still have their stockpiles for safekeeping, a kind of "just in case of emergency" option. The question is: Just how secure are these weapons? We know, for example, that nuclear weapons small enough to can fit into suitcases were developed in Russia, and some of them seem to have gone missing. Where did they go? Who has them?

Could a supply of deadly chemicals be stolen, and used on an unwitting population as part of a terrorist attack? And what about viruses? We know there are very dangerous viruses kept in topsecret government labs around the world, usually just for study. What if someone were able to get in and release one, or threatened to do it? What if it got out of their control? Could a terrorist attack meant only to scare people and get the terrorists what they want accidentally backfire, and wind up sickening and/or wiping out the entire population?

Cyberterrorism brings up another whole range of nightmares. We all know about hackers and what they can do, and some are deliberately trying to get into the most protected sites and systems you can think of. Some just want to prove they can do it, but others really want to cause damage. Hackers might be trying to find codes to launch nuclear weapons, for example, or find ways to disable power grids and shut down all the electricity in a region, or even a whole country. A group of terrorist hackers that really knows what they're doing might be bring a whole country to its knees. Could they even take over the whole world this way? Or could they accidentally unleash something they didn't mean to, and destroy the internet or all power systems? What would happen if they did?

AI GONE AWRY

MOVIES AND TELEVISION SHOWS about intelligent robots are very popular. From *Star Trek* to *Star Wars* and so many between those classics, robots and androids have been entertaining science fiction fans for decades. And although these amazing creations are still only imaginary, advances in technology are getting better each day. Robots *do* exist in the real world, and can do amazing things, like work in places that are too dangerous for humans to go (underwater, in space, and so on).

At the same time, people have been trying to create robots and/or computers that not only move, but also think. The term is *artificial intelligence*, or AI, is one of the main goals of many scientists in robotics, but what does it mean? Well, it would be a creation that is as complex as a human brain, and so could literally think for itself. This "brain" might not exist inside of a robot body at all. It might be a gigantic computer contained in a big box.

But what would it really mean? A true AI would be conscious. In other words, it would be aware of itself and others. It would have an identity of its own, just like we all do. And that's the tricky part. How would we know if and when this supercomputer became self-aware? Even if it told us, that might not be true; it might just be saying what it was programmed to say. To be truly intelligent, it would have to think for itself and form ideas that were not put into it by programmers.

Way back in 1950, English mathematician Alan Turing created a game, later deemed the "Turing test," that could be used to see if a machine

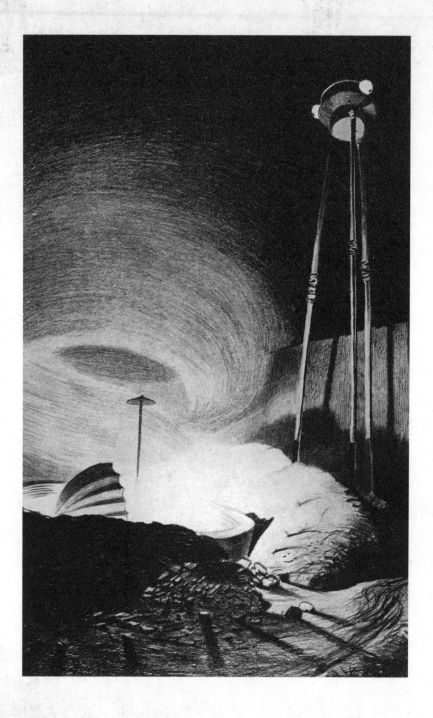

A HISTORY OF THE END OF THE WORLD

could think. It involves having a human ask a computer and another human a series of questions, without knowing which set of answers comes from the human, and which comes from the machine. This test is repeated many times to build up a set of answers. If the questioner can't determine who is human and who is the machine in more than half of the answers, the machine might be intelligent.

There have been other AI tests formulated over the years, but some scientists doubt that we could ever know if a computer can truly think for itself.

What's the danger in all of this? Suppose that programmers are able to make an artificial brain, a computer so complex that it can think and behave on its own. And what if, as it learns more and more, it decides that it is superior to the humans that created it and doesn't need them anymore? This exact story has been the subject of many popular films, including the *Terminator* and the *Matrix* film series. AIs take over the world, and either wipe out humanity, or use them as slaves and/or fuel.

We're all pretty familiar with the concept, but how likely is it? At the moment, probably not very. But advances in computers are happening every day, and many scientists feel that it's only a matter of time before an actual thinking machine is created. What will happen then? Will it be nice, or will it be evil? Will there be safety precautions in place to turn it off if it decides to turn against us?

THE SINGULARITY

RELATED TO AI IS THE CONCEPT of the *singularity*. Vernor Vinge, a mathematics professor, coined the term in the 1980s, but the idea has been around for a long time, and many others have talked about this important, and potentially scary, event. In 1993, Vinge wrote, "Within thirty years, we will have the technological means to create superhuman intelligence. Shortly after, the human era will be ended. ... I think it's fair to call this event a singularity."

In other words, Vinge believes we will soon make machines that are superior to us. In one sense, our old world will end. If and when this happens, we will be exposed to the dangers mentioned in the previous section: AIs that have the ability to decide they no longer need us, make war on us, and so on. But even if we don't have to face that, other dangers could change our world forever.

The super-machines may decide that they still need us, but may make us their slaves, perhaps in a way we are not even aware of. Think of the *Matrix* movies for one horrifying example.

Our civilization would almost certainly be turned upside down. If everything is done by robots, what is our purpose? Why let humans do the work when a machine could do it better and faster? We would have outlived our usefulness, except maybe as slaves.

Related to slavery, we might accidentally create a thinking machine that wants to do what it thinks is best for its human creators, and so creates a dictatorship that forces us to do everything it wants, "for our own good." The machine might really think it is doing something good, but rob us of our freedom, our free will, of anything and everything that makes us human, just so we can fit into the role that the machine says is optimal.

Or we may realize that the best thing for us to do is to make ourselves more machinelike, so that we can also be more intelligent, stronger, and better able to keep pace with this new superintelligence. Computer chips in the brain, implants in organs, things to make our muscles stronger; how long before the human race would become a species of cyborgs? To see how badly this could turn out, you only need to think of the Borg on *Star Trek*: living beings that have willingly merged with machines and now try to force others to do the same ... resistance is futile!

The AIs might want to merge together to create a super-brain. They would need more and more resources to do this, and might destroy the world to get all the material they needed, with the idea of creating a vast thinking computer that was the size of a planet.

Despite all of these fearsome potentialities, there are many who hope for the Singularity, and think that it has the chance to bring about the end to a lot of our problems. Which will be our fate? Who knows?

NANOBOTS/GRAY GOO

SIMILAR TO AI GONE CRAZY, this hypothetical idea suggests that if we're not careful, very tiny machines could do us in! You may have heard of nanotechnology, which is the use of very small robots and machines to perform tasks that are difficult for us much larger humans. The idea is that these microscopic bots can be sent into places to do work that we can't. They could be useful in everything from surgeries to cleaning up the environment. In fact, nanotechnology is already here, and used for these jobs. But there could be a downside to it, according to some scientists.

The problem could come if these microbots were also programmed to self-replicate, in other words, to make copies of themselves to continue their work when some of them wore out, or if more of them were needed for a job. Let's say, for example, a group of molecule-size machines were set out to help clean up a toxic waste spill, and are programmed to "eat" the material and clear the area. That all sounds good. But what if, when they were done, they didn't stop "eating" everything in sight? What if they were programmed to make copies of themselves and the programming couldn't be turned off? Or, even worse, what if they somehow learned to make copies of themselves without us telling them to?

So, these tiny robots go to work and finish the job. If they start making copies of themselves and find that there is no more toxic waste to consume, they could simply start devouring anything and everything around them. As they consume more and more, the need for more of them grows, so they "give birth" to more copies of themselves and go on to destroy even more of the surrounding environment.

This self-replication isn't just a few bots here and there; it multiplies with each new generation of robots—two make four, four make eight, eight make sixteen, and so on. And if they've been programmed, or we lose control of them, suddenly there would be billions, even trillions, of them eating everything in their path. They would be able to consume everything on Earth in a matter of days, leaving nothing but dust and rock. And they might even be able to gobble up that, too, until there was nothing left but space rocks and hot magma that becomes solid in the cold vacuum of space. We'd be completely gone, and there would be nothing we could do to stop it.

Or even worse, what if someone got hold of this technology, and tried to use it as a weapon? They could accidentally unleash total destruction.

This is a scary idea! But how likely is it? Thank goodness, not very. Some of the scientists who first warned about the possibility have admitted that much. Simply programming in the right controls would be enough to stop it from happening. But it shows that we have to be careful as we invent new technologies, because dangers we never thought about could arise.

DELETING THE SIMULATION

HERE'S THE THING: This world, this solar system, the whole universe? It might not be real. Obviously, it's real in the sense that we can see and perceive it, but the underlying structure may be something very different than we perceive. Scientists and others have been thinking about this for a long time. Because we can create imaginary worlds, video games, simulations, and so on, what is the chance that our own universe might be someone else's simulation?

It sounds like a ridiculous proposition, because we are all very sure that we are who we are, that this world is real, and when we go to, say, play a video game, we can see that the world on the screen is something made-up, a clever combination of programming and technology. That may be true, but what are the chances that we are *also* a clever creation of programming and someone else's technology? Strangely, it's not as impossible as it sounds.

We assume we are living in "base" reality; in other words, we assume that we are real and can imagine other realities that are not. So, we can make up video games and simulations and enjoy them, because they're not real. We can even imagine a time when we could create a simulation so realistic that it would seem like we were really living in it. Think of how fun it would be to play in a video game where you are surrounded on all sides by monsters or aliens that seem absolutely real, and you could interact with them as if you were in that space. Many programmers think it won't be too long before we have those types of immersive games.

So, if *we* can create something like this, what's to say that another civilization already hasn't, maybe a long time ago? What if *we* are the simulation that someone else is letting run on its own, just to see how it plays out? It gets even worse: What if the technological civilization that built our simulation is *also* a simulation made by an even earlier group of mysterious beings? What if many of these simulations are nested inside of each other? If we manage to create a truly realistic simulation, it might just be the latest in a long line of fake realities that keeps inventing new ones! It's a mind-boggling thought, and there probably isn't any way to prove it's true. Right?

Well, some smart people have done the math, and one of the more shocking conclusions is that there is about a 50-50 chance that we *are* a simulation! That's right, the chance that we are not real is a coin flip!

Which brings up a very unpleasant thought: What if whoever created this simulation decides to end it? Maybe they get bored, want to improve it, start over, etc., so they just switch it off. Our world and our whole universe would come to an end, and we'd have no warning. We'd just all be gone one day, and that would be it.

Now, not everyone accepts this 50-50 chance; in fact, many have argued that we are definitely the base reality. But they can't prove it. So, every night you go to sleep, just recognize that there's a chance everything could get switched off, and you'll never wake again.

GENETIC ENGINEERING

GENETIC ENGINEERING IS THE PROCESS of changing the gene makeup of living organisms to obtain results that benefit the organism. Probably the best example at the moment is the genetic modification of crops to make them more resistant to insects, droughts, disease, and so on, or to make them grow larger and provide more nutrition. On paper, this seems like a good idea, and the practice has produced some very good results. But many people are worried about it getting out of hand and producing unforeseen consequences.

What if seeds from genetically modified crops were scattered into new fields where they shouldn't be? What if, after a few growing seasons, something started to go wrong and the crops stop yielding good food, or they begin to grow smaller and die? People against genetic modification say that there are too many risks to continue with this until we have a better understanding of what will happen in the long term. Those who support engineering say that it can potentially feed millions of people, improve nutrition, make better use of land and soil, and improve lives. It's obviously a complex question, and we're a long way from having definitive answers.

An even bigger problem facing scientists is genetically modifying humans. Again, the idea would be to go in and change certain genes to make it less likely that someone would inherit a genetic disease. Would it be possible to remove some terrible problems from humanity with the right kind of engineering? Some people think so. Looking at the human genome, they say, could someday allow us to remove the problems we don't want and make the human race better overall.

But would we really be better? What if something goes wrong? It's almost certain that some mistake would be made while we're trying to get it just right. What if the wealthy and powerful decide to start modifying their children to have extra intelligence, extra strength, and so on, and keep that knowledge for themselves? What would happen to everyone else? Would a new, subspecies of superhumans who could do anything they wanted and not be stopped arise? Would "regular" humans just die off over time, or would they be kept and used as menial labor or slaves to do all the tasks the superhumans didn't want to do? Could the military try to create super soldiers that enjoy unnatural strength and endurance? What if they accidentally create people who are very strong, but also amplify anger and aggression in the process? What if they accidentally create monsters that can't be controlled?

As you can see, there are some big ethical questions here, and many people hope that governments will ban certain types of genetic engineering in humans. But, as with biological warfare, this won't stop some groups from trying to create the next best thing.

ISAAC NEWTON AND THE YEAR 2060

THE ENGLISHMAN ISAAC NEWTON (1642–1727) is known today as a scientist, one of the most important in human history, in fact. He developed ideas about physics and the laws of motion, created the mathematical discipline of calculus (which many high school students hate him for), and was one of the key thinkers at the beginning of the Scientific Revolution.

Everyone knows the story about Newton sitting under an apple tree and an apple falling on his head, which then gave him ideas about gravity. The true story seems to be that the apple didn't hit him on the head. Instead, while watching an apple fall, he began to wonder why it fell down and not sideways, or in some other direction. Newton figured out that something must be pulling it, and everything else, toward Earth.

Although Newton's reputation as a scientist is well known, a lot of people don't know that he was also very interested in subjects like alchemy (and its never-ending quest to turn other metals into gold), magic, and prophecy. These are subjects that no serious scientist now would touch with a ten-foot pole! But Newton existed in a different age, one where some scientists still liked studying these kinds of topics. Newton was also a devout Christian and frequently looked to the Bible to try and interpret its meaning. He was also interested in—you guessed it—the end of the world.

Through a series of fairly complex calculations that resembled a scientific or mathematical formula, Newton tried to work out when, approximately, the end of the world would happen. He firmly believed that no one could ever know the exact date; that was for God alone. But he could use the knowledge he had to work out a "ballpark" figure. And so he did: the world would end, but not before the year 2060. Why this year? Well, it's a bit complicated to sum up concisely. In any case, he wrote:

"It [the world] may end later, but I see no reason for its ending sooner [than 2060]. This I mention not to assert when the time of the end shall be, but to put a stop to the rash conjectures of fancifull men who are frequently predicting the time of the end, and by doing so bring the sacred prophesies into discredit as often as their predictions fail."

In other words, he only did it so that others would stop making silly predictions that would fail. Of course, this didn't stop that at all!

Newton didn't go into detail about what he thought would happen, so we don't have any descriptions of apocalyptic destruction or death. Instead, he simply wanted to offer a possible date and leave it at that. Now, because his predictions were based on complex interpretations of the Bible that he came up with, it's highly likely that the year 2060 will come and go, just like every other predicted year, and nothing much will happen. Then again, Newton *did* say the end might happen later than that ...

MALTHUSIAN CATASTROPHE

ALTHOUGH IT MAY SOUND LIKE the title of a disaster movie, it's actually a theory that was first put forward by Thomas Robert Malthus (1766–1834), a scholar and expert on economics and population. Malthus studied the way that groups of people live together and how the population grows over time. He said that it was only natural for populations to increase, but that this came with several problems. Basically, no matter what we do, nature will self-correct at some point.

He believed that if people are happy and well fed, the population will double about once every twenty-five years. Unfortunately, the production of food will not keep up with that pace. We can ignore this problem and keep expanding into new areas to produce more food, but at some point, we will run out of space and the math will catch up with us: we will have too many people and not enough to feed them.

At that point, nature takes over and there is a large die-off until the population dwindles to a level where there will be enough for everyone to eat again. Malthus saw this as a cycle recurring throughout world history, of populations growing and then shrinking as too many people (or other animals) make unreasonable demands on natural resources. Eventually, something has to give, and it will always be a population, not nature!

This is a controversial theory, and a lot, if not most, economists and other scientists don't believe it today. There are ways to use technology, for example, to improve crops and allow more people to be fed with less land and labor. So, for the time being, this is not a problem. Further, they say, the human population is not doubling every twenty-five years. Since 1800, when there were one billion people on the planet, the population has grown to about 7.5 billion. Between 1927 and 1974 (47 years), the population doubled from two billion to four billion. But it will be 2023 (49 years) before the population has doubled again.

The population is expected to stabilize at about ten to twelve billion people by the year 2100, and this may prove that, yes, there is a number

over which we can't expand. Some researchers have warned that realistically, Earth can only support about 1.5 billion people living at the "Western" standard of life, and that for everyone, life will have to become much simpler and less wasteful if we are to survive in the centuries ahead.

Whether or not Malthus was right, we have to look at population as one of the important factors in how life on Earth can continue.

THE BIG RIP

THERE ARE MANY THEORIES about how the world might end, but what about the universe itself? What could bring even this vast, mysterious universe to an end? Well, there are a few ideas out there, and to be honest, they all sound pretty unpleasant. One of the more popular theories going around these days is the idea of the "big rip."

We know that since the big bang, the universe and everything in it is expanding. Galaxies are flying through endless space, getting farther and farther away from one another, even if we can't observe the motion in real time, because it's a very drawn-out process. But this movement seems to be speeding up. The theory is that the pull of this expansion will at some point become stronger than the gravity inside of it, and if this happens, everything will be ripped apart by dark energy (energy that is believed to exist in the universe, but that we can't see because it's, well, dark).

If this energy is able to overcome what it affects, it could literally tear everything to shreds, leaving a universe populated with countless single atoms. Nothing would stick together to form stars, planets, or string cheese. It would be a universe of endless dark, filled with unthinkable numbers of particles darting around, unable to get together and do anything interesting.

It's a rather horrible thought, but what are the chances it could happen? Actually, scientists aren't sure. But it is a theory that astronomers, physicists, and others take seriously. Fortunately for us, this massive universal rip isn't going to happen any time soon, if it ever does. We'll be long gone before everything starts to get torn apart, and it's just as well, because experiencing it in real time would not be fun!

THE BIG CRUNCH

MOST PEOPLE KNOW about the big bang, the theory that the universe began with an explosion. Over time, the universe grew from this explosion, and everything we see, from planets and stars to whole galaxies, is sprinting through space because of it.

We know that galaxies are moving farther and farther away—knowledge provided because of an effect called the Doppler shift. This means that the light stars and such give off shifts and changes color over time. It's the same effect as when you hear a car drive by playing music. You'll notice that the music gets lower in pitch the farther away the car gets from you. This has nothing to do with the music, but rather, how the sound waves move through the air. The same principle applies to light.

So, if there was a big bang, and the universe is expanding, and things are flying away from one another, will it just go on forever? Some scientists think that, yes, everything will just get farther and farther apart until it is so far away it will barely be possible to see anything at all. Space, after all, is infinite.

But others think that at some point, everything will begin to fall back inward, until it all "crunches" back down into an infinitely small space, which will lead to another big bang. Obviously, by the time this actually happens, we and our planet will be long gone, but it's an interesting theory about a bigger end than just our little world.

Interestingly, the idea of a universe that expands and contracts is a familiar concept in the Hindu religion, which sees the cosmos as having cycles. There are stories of Brahman (the absolute, the one) who "breathes" the universe in and out, so that an exhale is the universe living and expanding, while an inhale is the universe contracting back to its source. When you think about it, the big bang and the big crunch don't seem too different from that!

Most astronomers, however, don't believe this crunch will happen. The evidence for it doesn't seem to be there, and a more probable fate for the universe looks to be something equally unpleasant sounding, known as ... heat death (see the next entry).

THE BIG FREEZE: THE HEAT DEATH OF THE UNIVERSE

MANY ASTRONOMERS NOW BELIEVE that the fate of the universe will be rather dark: they expect the universe to keep expanding forever, for all of the energy in it to be used up until there is literally nothing left. Long after Earth is gone, the stars will burn out, the quasars will stop pulsing, and there will be no more light (though maybe still black holes). The universe will become an unimaginably black, empty void.

How long would it take to get to this state? Some calculations say it could be as long as 10^{106} years, which is ten multiplied by itself 106 times! That is a *very* long time!

But even then, it might not be the end. Some studies suggest that the universe is actually getting hotter, not cooler, so it may be that this "dark age" will never happen. Even if it did, there are also some calculations that show that energy productions could start up again and produce a new universe (though most think this probably wouldn't happen).

The final fate of the universe is unknown, and none of us will be around to see it (thank goodness!), but it's an almost sure bet that our tiny world will be long gone before it happens. That doesn't mean that millions of other worlds might not exist between now and then, with millions of other inhabitants wondering about where they came from and where they're going. The same questions we ask ourselves may be puzzling untold numbers of other beings on other planets throughout the cosmos, as they try to understand the vast, bizarre, sometimes frightening, and truly mysterious universe we call home.

SCIENCE

CHAPTER 3
CONSPIRACIES, SUPERSTITIONS, AND FAILED PREDICTIONS

AS YOU'VE PROBABLY GUESSED, a frightening subject like the end of the world has inspired many wild ideas, stories, and theories over the centuries. Some of them might seem believable, whereas others just seem ridiculous! A lot of them have popped up in the last fifty years or so, as people began to feel more and more uneasy about the momentum of the modern world, and the approach of the year 2000.

Even with that momentous date now past, belief in some kind of global catastrophe remains common. A lot of people have written a lot of books—and probably made a lot of money—about a number of apocalyptic ideas, some crazy, some frighteningly plausible.

This section looks at some of these theories, and also explores the unsettling concept of "doomsday cults," small religious groups that have staked much of their existence around the approaching end of the world, an obsession that often produces terrible and tragic ends for their own members.

Finally, for a bit of fun, we'll look at a whole lot of predictions about the end of the world that didn't come true, leaving those who believed in and promoted them feeling pretty foolish when the dates came and went.

Despite these failures, large numbers of people continue to offer up their own ideas about how and when it's going to happen. Just because everyone before them has been wrong doesn't mean that they're going to be discouraged!

THE POLE SHIFT

THE EARTH IS ACTUALLY a giant magnet. Thanks to the churning of molten material in the planet's core, a powerful magnetic field is generated, keeping deadly radiation from the sun and space away from us. This magnetic field is also why we have a North Pole and a South Pole. Actually, there are two North Poles: there's the geographic North Pole, which, along with the South Pole, marks where Earth spins on its axis. But there is also a magnetic north pole, which is a bit farther south, and moves around. In fact, it's moving faster than normal of late, and has traveled hundreds of miles across northern Canada over the last 150 years or so.

This is caused by competing magnetic forces deep inside Earth, and for many scientists, it's a troubling sign that the poles may be about to flip; north will become south, and south will become north. Scientists know that the poles have shifted many times during Earth's long history. The last time was about 780,000 years ago. As the poles are expected to shift about every 300,000 years, we're well overdue!

It *will* happen again, but what will happen? It will probably cause a lot of disruption to electronics and power grids, perhaps even blowing them out and sending us back to a less technological time. Scientists also worry that this could disrupt the magnetic field enough to leave certain parts of Earth more vulnerable to radiation … for hundreds or even thousands of years. People living in those areas might have to leave for their own safety.

That's the scientific point of view, but according to some conspiracy theorists, the threat from this shift is a lot bigger. Many seem to link this shift to a big disruption in Earth's crust, causing massive earthquakes, tidal waves, and worse, which will be devastating for population centers around the world. One theory holds that the continents could literally slide across the crust of the Earth and move rapidly to other locations. As we saw on page 58, some think that Antarctica was once the lost continent of Atlantis, and a crustal displacement sent it sliding down to where the South Pole now is. Of course, most say this is nonsense, but it's popular idea in conspiracy groups.

The poles will shift at some point in the future. Whether that's in a month or thousands of years, we just don't know. We do know that a pole shift will cause a lot of problems, but we don't quite know how bad they will be. Will the shift send the continents sliding around and basically destroy civilization as we know it? Probably not, but then again, we can't be 100 percent sure …

2012 AND THE MAYA CALENDAR

THE MAYA CALENDAR was all the rage a few years ago. Before 2012, a whole lot of people were talking about it, what it meant, what it might predict, and what would happen when it "ended." The biggest worry for some people was that on or around December 21, 2012, the world would end because the Maya calendar "predicted" it. The idea appeared everywhere: in books, TV shows, movies, and social media. Well, as you can see, we're all still here (I think; see page 115), so something must have been lost in translation. What was/is the Maya calendar, and why did so many people think it was so important?

The Maya were a people who created a great civilization in southern Mexico and nearby areas long before the Conquest. The civilization was at its most powerful between about 250 and 900 CE, when the Maya built great cities and monuments, and developed a complex and sophisticated calendar. After the year 900, political and social problems led to the civilization's decline, and some cities were abandoned. By the time the Spanish conquerors arrived in the sixteenth century, Maya civilization had weakened to the point of vanishing, despite some of its people living on.

One of the Mayas' great achievements was their calendar, which counted time in very large blocks. It makes use of what is called the long count, and it groups time into baktun (144,000 days). Thirteen *baktun* are one long count, or cycle. So what does this mean? Simply that a cycle lasts for about 5,126 years before coming to an end. People who studied the calendar claimed that the cycle would end on December 21, 2012. If that was the end of the calendar, did it mean that it was also the end of the world?

Some people who studied it thought so. They believed that the end of the calendar would mean a global cataclysm of some kind, ending civilization and forcing humanity to start over with the next cycle. Others thought a planet or asteroid might hit Earth. Still others thought there would be widespread flooding, or a shift in the poles. Many people

had many different theories, but doomsday predictors were all pretty sure that December 21 was *the* date to keep an anxious eye on.

So, what happened? Well, nothing, as you probably deduced. It turns out that these people interpreted the calendar incorrectly. Other scholars showed that the end of that baktun simply meant the start of another one, the way December becomes January, with nothing especially bad happening. Some even think that the date was wrong and the baktun ended earlier than 2012. And because the Maya civilization eventually collapsed, it strikes some people as very strange that they could predict the end of the world so far in the future, but not see their own doom coming.

People descended from the Maya have confirmed that those viewing the calendar as an apocalyptic warning were misguided, saying it was never meant to be a prediction of the world ending. As usual, it would have been better if the people excited by the calendar listened to those better positioned to understand it, instead of making up their own wild stories?

———————————

DID THE WORLD ALREADY END IN 2012?

HOT ON THE HEELS of the Maya calendar mix-up, some people don't see it as a failure, or a misinterpretation. Some believe that the world actually did end in 2012, just as predicted, only no one noticed.

Wait, what?

If this makes no sense to you, you're not alone. The explanation is a bit weird, but some people out there really think it could be true. According to the theory, the world came to an end, not because of planetary alignments, or erupting volcanoes, or zombies, or anything else, but because of an accident at the CERN Large Hadron Collider in Switzerland. Scientists use this massive structure to search for subatomic particles and to study things at sizes so small it's hard to even determine if they exist.

According to this conspiracy theory, in 2012, while scientists were looking for a particle called the Higgs boson, CERN accidentally created a black hole big enough to swallow Earth (remember the black hole threat from the "Science" chapter?). But scientists, using an advanced technology unknown to most, were able to save us by creating a simulation Earth, basically like one in a video game (remember the simulation theory from the "Science" chapter? Head back to page 115). And we never even noticed; we just woke up one day in a simulation without knowing everything had ended and that our "new" existence was a fake one.

Others go further and say that the world didn't "really" end in 2012, but in 2020, because of a calendar mix-up. You see, we've just been counting it wrong all these centuries: 2020 is really 2012 . So, yes the world ended, but it was in June 2020, and once again, we didn't even notice, just kept going right along as though nothing had happened.

Now, 2020 was a terrible year for much of the world, but still— nothing suggested that an artificial black hole ate Earth and we all just continued on as digital copies! On the other hand, given how many weird and awful things did happen in 2020, maybe we're now living in a simulation where the people controlling it are still just messing with us? If so, they need to stop!

As you can see, this is getting pretty ridiculous. Chances are, the world didn't get eaten up in either 2012 or 2020, and we're not in some crazy video game, thinking we're all still alive. But enough people believe it might be possible that they're willing to go online and talk it over. Such speculations are fun, but when it comes to way-out-there conspiracy theories like this, you have to take them with a pretty big grain of salt.

NOSTRADAMUS'S PREDICTIONS

A VERY POPULAR FIGURE in the history of doomsday prediction is Michel de Nostradame, known as Nostradamus. He was a sixteenth-century French doctor who wrote a book called *The Prophecies*, which first appeared in 1555. In it, he included many predictions about the future. Some of these seem to be very accurate and have been used by believers to prove that Nostradamus could indeed see the future. Others say that his writing is so vague and cryptic that his projections could be interpreted just about any way someone wished, making it look like Nostradamus was predicting a future event when he's really not communicating much of anything at all.

It was said that Nostradamus would fill a bowl with water and herbs and spend his nights gazing into it, trying to catch a glimpse of the future. He went into a kind of trance when he did this, and would have visions, which he would then write down. Nostradamus was a bit fearful of getting in trouble with church and government authorities for making his predictions, so he wrote them down in four-line verses called quatrains, which were composed in a mixture of languages so that they would be hard to read for many people, and subject to different interpretations by those who could.

Not only did Nostradamus avoid getting in trouble, he was invited by princes and kings to serve at their courts. He used a mixture of astrology, his own predictions, and readings of existing predictions to forecast what would happen. His followers today believe that he accurately predicted the French Revolution, the rises of Napoleon and Hitler, the assassination of John F. Kennedy, and even the September 11 attacks in New York.

Others think he just got lucky, made educated guesses, or wrote things in such a way that they could be interpreted as prophecies to someone intent on seeing them that way. Others think that he was actually making comments about the people and situations of his own time and disguising them as predictions about the future, so as not to get himself in trouble.

As for the end of the world? Well, of course Nostradamus had something to say about that! At least, some think so. People have been using his words to try to prove that the world was going to end for a long time, including in the year 2000, and yes, 2012. Almost every year, someone comes forward to claim that one of the cryptic quatrains proves that *this* is the year, at last! But so far, those claims have fallen flat. Some who have studied his work say that he claimed the world would finally end, but not until the year 3797. If that's the case, we can all breathe a little easier.

PLANETARY ALIGNMENT

EIGHT PLANETS ROTATE around our sun (since Pluto was demoted) at different speeds. The farther out a planet is, the longer it takes for it to make one complete rotation around our star. So, one year on Earth is shorter than one year on Mars, which is shorter than one on Jupiter, and so on. This means that the planets will be in different places in the solar system and in the night sky at any given time of the year. But

once in a while, something interesting happens, and two or more of the planets align.

A similar thing happens when we have an eclipse, where the moon lines up in front of Earth to temporarily block out the sun. These events were probably very mysterious and caused a lot of fear in earlier days, before people understood why they were happening. Why would the sun go away during the daytime, even if only for a short period of time?

As we learned more about the planets and their rotations, we saw that planets can do this, too. Sometimes it's just two planets, but occasionally, three or more can get in a single-file line. This obviously doesn't happen too often, so what does it mean? Well, not much, other than it's kind of an interesting thing to see. But that hasn't stopped those with busy imaginations from attributing some wild potentialities to the phenomenon.

One of the biggest fears is that somehow this alignment will result in extra gravity pulling on Earth and causing widespread destruction as tides go crazy, earthquakes become common, and chaos becomes general. Many people warned that December 21, 2012, was the big planetary alignment, and that this would bring the predicted Maya calendar end. And as we know, nothing happened. Like, nothing at all.

The fact is that the planets are simply too small and too far away from each other to have any real effect on one another. Even if five or six of them functionally aligned (and it can happen), there's just too much space between them for there to be any problems.

Part of the reason people don't understand how much space there is between the planets is our reliance on maps of the solar system that show the planets being far closer than they actually are. A few online sites have created accurate maps of the distance between the planets, where you have to scroll through the screen from one to the next, and it's absolutely mind-boggling, and anxiety-relieving, to see how far away they really are from each other!

ALIEN INVASION

THE IDEA THAT WE'RE NOT ALONE in the universe has intrigued people since long before modern times, and countless individuals have wondered what it might be like to meet beings from another planet, another star system, even another galaxy. Would they be anything like us? Or would they be so different that we might not even be able to tell if they were actually alive? And the most important questions: Would they be friendly, or hostile? If they weren't friendly, could we do anything to defend ourselves and our planet?

There are plenty of science fiction stories about future Earths where cordial relationships between humans and aliens exist (*Star Trek*, for example), but the idea that our visitors might be evil has fascinated and terrified people for a very long time. H. G. Wells's famous work, *The War of the Worlds*, published in 1897, told of Martians coming to our planet to take it over. Humanity is helpless against them, and the only thing that saves us is that these Martians have no immunity to earthly diseases, which kill them off.

There have been many versions of this tale over the years. Plenty of movies in the 1950s explored the idea of aliens visiting us, some good, some not so good. In most cases, humanity simply doesn't have the technology to fight off aliens in any kind of traditional battle, and so has to resort to unorthodox methods to defeat them.

These books, movies, TV shows, and video games make for great entertainment. But how likely is it that aliens invade Earth? There have been many theories over the years that an alien invasion was just about to happen, or was stopped by a secret, last-minute deal. Because we have no way of proving these assertions, we have to assume that they're likely untrue.

But given the immense size of the universe, it seems likely that other forms of life are out there, and that some could have developed technologies advanced enough to traverse the great distances in space. If they happened to notice us, they might come here. Why? Well, they

might need Earth's natural resources (minerals, water, and so on). Or they might be "collecting" planets to add to their empire. Worse, they might need slaves for work, or even (gulp!) food!

The thing is, some of these frightening theories are probably correct: if we were to encounter a species capable of traveling far enough to reach us, they would probably have technologies that would seem almost like magic to us, including their weapons. It's likely that we wouldn't be able to put up much of a resistance at all, and would easily be conquered.

So, do we need to worry about this? Probably not. But the great astronomer Stephen Hawking warned that we should probably stop broadcasting the fact of our existence out to the universe, because we have no idea who might answer! Such aliens may see us as weak, useless, easy to defeat, and we would be basically inviting them to come and take us over.

REPTILIAN OVERLORDS

ACCORDING TO SOME CONSPIRACY THEORISTS, Earth already *has* been conquered—a long time ago, in fact—by an evil species of intelligent lizards. These mysterious and dangerous aliens, said to be from the Alpha Draconis star system, have been on Earth for thousands of years, and have been slowly and secretly controlling civilization the entire time from their underground bases. There, they keep a collection of humans—some for slaves, the rest for food.

But they don't just remain in the dark. They are capable of shape-shifting and making themselves look completely human. While posing as humans, they have been able to infiltrate the highest levels of society and gain control of everything. Most could never tell a reptilian from a human, but people who have seen them in human forms claim that sometimes their disguises fail for a moment, and a flicker of a reptile-

like eye or a long tongue can be seen. People have even posted videos online that allege these reptilian disguises failing have been caught on camera. Most have been proven to be camera tricks and special effects, but many continue to insist that some of the footage is genuine.

The reptilian theory is most loudly supported by David Icke, who has written several books on the topic. And although many consider him to be more than a bit kooky, Icke insists that he's telling the truth and that he can prove it (though he has yet to provide any real, convincing proof).

So, who are some of the famous people and politicians that Icke thinks are reptilian aliens in disguise? He thinks that they have been in many royal families over the centuries, including the current British royals. He also thinks that in America, political figures like the Bush family (including President George H. W. Bush and George W. Bush), as well as the Clintons and Barack Obama are secretly lizard people who have gained power and influenced world events to meet their sinister designs. Among celebrities, Madonna, Katy Perry, and even Angelina Jolie have been identified as lizards in disguise.

Now, if this is all sounding pretty silly to you, you're in good company. But that doesn't stop a lot of people from believing it and posting their stories and theories on the internet. It's likely all nonsense. But if they do happen to be right, civilization as we know it (or would like it to be) ended a long time ago, and we're all just slaves living under a system we don't even know exists.

THE HOLLOW EARTH

FOR THOUSANDS OF YEARS, humans have wondered about the possibility of other worlds existing beneath our own. Could whole civilizations, even whole species, live in great cities and communities under the earth, unknown to us?

Explorers have actually set out to find ways into this subterranean realm, with some suggesting that the entrances are at the North and South Poles, which is why it is so hard for people to get to them.

Conspiracy theorists have imagined that all sorts of unknown species are living in the caverns under the earth, and not all of them are good. Believers in the reptilians say that they have bases, and even whole cities, underground (see page 145). There they control humanity without us even knowing it. UFOs, some claim, are not coming from other planets, but are evidence of the advanced technology belonging to the beings that live beneath us. They send these ships out from time to time to spy on us and see what we're up to.

What do these underground dwellers have to do with the end of the world? Well, some say these beings hate us so much that they're obsessed with wiping us out and reclaiming the surface for themselves.

In the 1940s, a magazine called *Amazing Stories* published a series of stories by a man named Richard Sharpe Shaver, who claimed that under the earth a huge network of tunnels leads to cities populated by a species called the Dero. These are the descendants of a good people, the Tero, who became evil over thousands of years. The Dero have advanced technology and use their powers to control and harm humans all around the world. They also kidnap people to enslave or eat them. Shaver claimed they were biding their time, waiting for the right moment to act.

The author claimed that he had been kept as a prisoner by them for several years. Of course, many people thought it was all made up; *Amazing Stories* was a science fiction magazine, after all! But strangely, many others came forward with similar stories, saying they had been kidnapped by these beings, chased out of caves by them, or otherwise attacked. The story of the Dero still has a number of believers today.

Does an evil group of beings live beneath us, waiting for the day when they can destroy our civilization with their superior technology? Only time will tell ...

HAARP

NO, THIS IS NOT AN UNUSUAL version of the musical instrument. It's an acronym for "High-frequency Active Auroral Research Program," which the U.S. Air Force ran at a government site in Alaska. This strange-looking facility consisted of 180 antennae spread over forty acres. Officially, it was designed to study the weather and how particles behave in the part of the atmosphere known as the ionosphere. This is also the part of the atmosphere that helps radio transmissions travel from one place to another. Scientists felt that studying it could be helpful in gaining an understanding of the damaging effects solar flares may have on electronics and radio transmissions. The program was shut down in 2014.

But is that the whole story? (Cue sinister laugh.) There must be more to it, and conspiracies abound as to what was really going on up there. One problem is that the facility was secret, and only people with special clearance were allowed in. That level of secrecy must mean that the government was hiding something, right?

But what?

There are many theories about what the HAARP facility was up to, but the most popular ones are weather control, creating earthquakes, and mind control, all stratagems employed by the military to gain an advantage over their enemies. Think about it, if you can cause an earthquake under an enemy army, you could do serious damage. If you could create a terrible thunderstorm over them, you could bog them down in mud and water, and they'd be neutralized. Some accused the facility of working to create hurricanes that would bombard the coastlines of enemy countries. Of course, it would be best if you could control people's minds—then you could get them to do whatever you want!

Some people went so far as to suggest that HAARP experiments caused climate change. One of the things that HAARP was known to do was use its antennae to heat up a portion of the ionosphere to study certain particles. But if it's heating up the ionosphere, might that also cause problems with climate and weather? Is runaway global warming, which could bring the end of civilization, the result of some mad science experiments by the Air Force?

It's a terrifying idea, but one without any truth to it. Climate scientists pointed out that the total amount of energy generated by HAARP was far less than a single flash of lightning, of which there are hundreds, if not thousands, around the world every day. And simply nothing could affect the geology of Earth enough to cause it to rumble and quake. And as for mind control? How would a research facility in the far north be able to reach out and control what you think, thousands of miles away? No, HAARP wasn't responsible for helping bring about climate change to end the world, or anything else, but it makes for a really good story!

DOOMSDAY PREPPERS

THEY DON'T USUALLY MAKE HEADLINES, and they're not technically a cult like the groups covered in the next few entries. But a small, determined group of people are making preparations for the absolute worst-case scenario—hence the name "preppers." Politically, they tend to be on the Right, believing that the current social and economic situations in the world are unstable and will eventually come crashing down, one way or another.

Sometimes, they believe the end will be the result of a foreign attack: North Korea, Russia, and Iran are all popular choices to usher in the apocalypse. There was and is a genuine fear among some preppers that North Korea will be able to detonate an EMP (electromagnetic pulse) bomb above the United States that will knock out most, if not all, of our power grid, potentially killing millions and taking us back to the nineteenth century in terms of technology. When that happens, some of these preppers fear, we will be vulnerable to a foreign invasion. Others

fear that a full-scale nuclear war is still a threat, and that they have to make plans to ensure their survival in case that threat becomes reality.

What kinds of plans? The preppers are interested in anything that will make them self-sufficient, with no need to rely on outside sources for food, water, and protection. They have formed communities where they share ideas and, most important, products. A regular gathering called SurvivalCon allows for people and companies that sell survival products to fellow preppers. These include everything from shelters to special cases that can shield a person's phone and computer to protect them from an EMP attack. Packaged foods that don't spoil are another popular item, as well as seeds and other items for cultivating food.

There are also devices for purifying water and storing it safely. And of course, preppers want to have as many kinds of weapons available to them as possible, to fight off scavengers and enemies.

Elements of this movement seem like common sense. It's a good idea to have some food and water stored away in case of emergencies; the COVID-19 pandemic showed us that. It's also never a bad idea to learn how to grow food, or about safety and survival. But critics point out that a lot of talk in these groups sounds similar to what one would hear from a cult: seeing enemies everywhere, paranoia that certain groups are out to get them, blaming other groups for all of their problems, and so on.

Some preppers have crossed the line into violence, threatening their neighbors or local government if they feel their rights are not being respected. There is a definite crossover between some of these groups and those with extreme political beliefs, like neo-Nazi organizations. As with any group, how preppers choose to respond to the approaching end differs from person to person. But some of them seem to be a bigger threat to society than whatever end they're envisioning.

DOOMSDAY CULTS: HEAVEN'S GATE

IN MARCH 1997, the news reported a shocking story: thirty-nine members of an obscure group calling themselves Heaven's Gate were found dead near San Diego, California, having killed themselves at the request of their leader. The cult members seemed to have gone willingly, a stunning revelation that caused many around the world to look closer at this group and what they believed.

Heaven's Gate was founded in the 1970s by a nurse named Bonnie Lu Nettles, who soon after recruited Marshall Herff Applewhite. The pair cultivated a set of unusual beliefs and became convinced that: (1) the end of the world was coming soon; (2) they were actually aliens in human bodies, and that their alien race was the source of all religious belief on Earth.

They began to find others interested in their philosophy and gathered a group around them. Calling themselves "Do" (Applewhite) and "Ti" (Nettles), they convinced these followers to change their own names, adding the letters "DY" to the end of three other letters that made up their new names: TLLODY, CHKODY, SRRODY, and so on. These were their "true" names and proof that they too were aliens forced to live in human bodies. Both taught that in time, their bodies would be transformed into their natural forms, and then they would ascend to a starship that would take them to a kind of alien heaven. The group members saw themselves as caterpillars, waiting to become butterflies. Only, there was a problem: in 1985, Bonnie Lu Nettles died of cancer. This was not at all what she and Applewhite had said would happen. They were supposed to transform in this life and become something better. So what happened? Had they lied?

Applewhite was determined to fix things before his followers deserted. He and Nettles had claimed they were already "perfect," but had chosen to live in human bodies to help others. Now Applewhite changed the story: the final stage of the transformation was actually death. The soul would undergo the last part of the change and become a perfect alien being that ascended to the stars. Obviously, this novel doctrine set the stage for the tragedy that occurred twelve years later.

By the mid-1990s, the cult was foundering, and Applewhite was having trouble finding new members. He decided that his "mission" was complete and that it was time to "ascend" to the next level. The end of the world was coming soon, he proclaimed, but Heaven's Gate members could escape and live forever. How? Applewhite claimed that a spaceship was hiding in the Hale-Bopp comet, which at that time was passing close by Earth. Applewhite used the astronomical event to spur on his followers, telling them that if they took their own lives, their souls would ascend to the ship in the comet, which would take them all to freedom.

In March 1997, his followers did what he asked and killed themselves by eating some poisoned applesauce or pudding. Applewhite also took his own life, which tells us that he likely believed what he was saying.

DOOMSDAY CULTS: AUM SHINRIKYO

THIS JAPANESE CULT was founded by Shoko Asahara in 1984. Asahara had a strong interest in both Christianity and Buddhism and wanted to put together something that fused ideas from both into his own brand of spirituality. He tried to get his new group, Aum Shinrikyo, recognized as an official religion by the Japanese government and was turned down at first. Asahara then appealed and was granted the distinction he desired.

For several years, the group attracted followers and Asahara became something of a celebrity in Japan. But what started as just another offshoot religious group began to take a sinister turn. It is not clear whether Asahara let everything go to his head, or whether he'd always planned to unveil himself, but in 1992, he said that he was Christ, and Japan's only "genuine" spiritual teacher. He even wrote a book called *Declaring Myself the Christ*, which is pretty cut and dry! Along with this, he believed that there were conspiracies against him and "true" spirituality everywhere, plots orchestrated by governments, the British royal family, other Japanese religions, and so on.

Asahara also began to proclaim that the end of the world was approaching and that he had the power to "take away sins" from those who wished to be saved before it did. A nuclear war started by the United States would occur in late 2003, the cult claimed, and anyone not saved by Asahara before then would be lost for eternity.

This sounds like typical cultish nonsense, built around the idea that a leader is the one person who can provide salvation. What happened next is anything but typical. At some point, Asahara interpreted various Buddhist scriptures to mean that he was justified in killing people who opposed the cult before they could accumulate bad karma, thus "saving" them. In the first few years of the 1990s, the cult began targeting people it viewed as inimical for assassination and succeeded in killing a few of these unfortunate souls. The group also began manufacturing sarin (a deadly nerve agent) and other nerve gases in secret, and although they had some successes (if you can call it that) and some failures while trying them out, the cult was able to keep itself out of the spotlight. The police suspected nothing from the group—that is, until March 1995.

During that month, the cult launched a chemical weapons attack on five trains in Tokyo's subway, killing thirteen people and severely injuring fifty-four. It's thought that up to 6,000 others were sickened by the attack. Investigations revealed that the Aum Shinrikyo cult was behind the attack, and the police arrested several of those involved, including Asahara (who was caught in May). But the group had planned more attacks. In April, a device containing cyanide was found in a busy train station. If it had been able to release its gas into the station's ventilation system, as many as 10,000 people could have been killed.

Asahara and several others were eventually executed for their crimes, and the group, which still exists, has denounced violence and purged its teachings of the idea that it needs to save people from themselves by killing them. A large improvement, perhaps, but not enough to escape Asahara's dark shadow as far as the Japanese government is concerned, as they continue to keep an eye on the Aum Shinrikyo.

DOOMSDAY CULTS:
ORDER OF THE SOLAR TEMPLE

THE ORIGINS OF THE Order of the Solar Temple are a bit unclear. Most think it was founded in 1984, but some suggest early versions of the group might have existed as far back as the early 1950s. In any case, OST was a Christian cult based in Switzerland that looked back to the Middle Ages, and especially to the Knights Templar, for inspiration.

The Knights Templar were founded in the twelfth century to assist the crusaders in the Holy Land. They were a monastic order, meaning that its members were monks, but they were also knights. Yes, it seems strange, because we usually envision monks as individuals who lead quiet, contemplative lives, grow herbs, and sing those somber Gregorian chants. The Templars did do these things, but they also suited up in armor and went out to fight as defenders of other Christians. They disappeared in the early 1300s, after a French king decided that he wanted all their money and brought phony charges against them. That's not a story for this book, though it is an interesting one.

In any case, OST took the Templars as inspiration, but incorporated some occult practices and good, old-fashioned sci-fi into their beliefs. They taught that the end of the world was coming soon, and that they would be able to assist in bringing order, given the structure of their group. First, there would be an ecological collapse; then Jesus would return as a "solar god-king" and recognize the OST among his faithful.

To be among that number, OST charged its members large fees, enabling its leaders to live lavishly. Some very wealthy people joined and gave the cult a lot of money for the opportunity to advance through the ranks and become senior members.

All of this might not have mattered much; con artists always find new ways to fleece people out of their money. Sure, it was a crime, but no one was being physically harmed—yet. As is usually the case with these kinds of mind-bending cults, things quickly became violent.

One of the cult's founders, Joseph Di Mambro, became upset that the group was beginning to lose popularity and members in the early 1990s. But what really pushed him over the edge was when one former member named a newborn son "Emmanuel," a name Di Mambro believed would be given to the reborn Christ, and which he had named his own son. He claimed that the child of these former members was in fact the Antichrist, and ordered that the whole family be murdered. Some of his followers carried out the crime, stabbing the ex-OSTs with a wooden stake.

Knowing that the end was near for him, Di Mambro then arranged for a ritual suicide for dozens of followers. More than seventy took their own lives or were murdered, after being told that their time on this planet was up, and that their spirits would go live on a planet orbiting the star Sirius. There were more mass deaths of cult members in the next year or two, but the predicted end of the world never came.

Amazingly, the cult was able to reorganize and slough off its chilling past and teachings. It still exists today, and has several hundred members.

DOOMSDAY CULTS: DAVID KORESH AND THE BRANCH DAVIDIANS

IN APRIL 1993, the U.S. government carried out a siege on a compound in Waco, Texas, at the Mount Carmel Center. Inside were almost a hundred devotees of a religious group called the Branch Davidians, which was led by a man named David Koresh. The group had been at a standoff with the government for fifty-one days over the issue of housing an illegal stash of weapons; this siege brought the impasse to an end, and a tragic one. A fire broke out (the cause has never been determined), and nearly eighty members of the group were killed, including Koresh.

Many people saw the group as nothing more than a dangerous cult, with Koresh as its even more dangerous leader, and had no sympathy for those that passed away.

The truth is a bit more complicated than that.

The Branch Davidians had existed since at least the 1950s, as a sect that broke away from the Seventh-day Adventist Church. Koresh, who was born in 1959, was a late comer to the group who took advantage of troubles in its leadership (including the then leader's claim that they were able to raise the dead!). Koresh was able to take control sometime around 1989. This makes the group slightly different from what is often thought of as a "cult," because Koresh was not the founder.

But it was soon obvious he was leading the group into dangerous territory. Koresh claimed to be a prophet, and then the messiah, and announced to the group that the end of the world was certain to arrive soon. He seems to have really believed it, too, stockpiling weapons in anticipation of the coming end times. Although Koresh wasn't just spouting apocalyptic predictions to gain power; he exploited people as well, insisting he had the right to marry more than one woman, and abusing a number of members.

When federal authorities got word that the group had acquired a large collection of potentially illegal weapons, they obtained a search warrant and went to Waco in February 1993. Of course, Koresh and the Davidians had no intention of letting them in; there was a shoot-out, during which six government agents and four Davidians were killed. After that, the group barricaded itself in, and the standoff began. Government forces tried many strategies to get the group to come out, including playing loud and obnoxious music at all hours. Koresh himself seemed willing to negotiate, but the standoff dragged on. Finally, the government tried to force the issue by pumping CS gas (a nonlethal agent commonly used in riot control) into the compound to force people out, while they battered down the doors and gates.

At some point, the fire broke out, and many people died, including twenty-one children under the age of sixteen. Many felt afterward that this use of force was too much, and that negotiations should have continued. Others have the sense that Koresh, disturbingly, got exactly what he wanted.

DOOMSDAY CULTS: THE TRUE RUSSIAN ORTHODOX CHURCH

FOR A GROUP CLAIMING to be the True Russian Orthodox Church, it was amazingly small. Based outside of the city of Penza in central Russia, the group mostly kept to themselves. Led by an eccentric man named Pyotr Kuznetsov, members were told to reject most modern things as the works of the devil. They were not allowed to listen to the radio, watch television, have credit cards, eat processed food, or even handle money, as all of these inventions were modern and therefore "sinful."

As you might imagine, this was not a very popular group, but it became famous for one incident. Like many other cult leaders, Kuznetsov was

convinced that the world would end soon—in May 2008, to be exact. But because he and his followers were the "true church," they needed to survive so they could lead the society that came afterward. And how were they supposed to weather the apocalypse? By hiding in a bunker contained within a big cave until it was all over.

In November 2007, about thirty of them headed underground, as instructed by their leader. Kuznetsov wasn't with his followers, having been arrested. In any case, the cult members did what he asked, and threatened to commit mass suicide if the authorities tried to intervene or force them to leave. They were fully ready to spend a Russian winter in a cave, because they believed so strongly in what Kuznetsov had told them!

The group's resolve was strong at first, but, as you might imagine, the novelty wore off quickly. By March, several members had had enough. Seven women emerged and were treated by doctors. A few days later, fourteen more came out of the cave, because melting snow had caused part of it to collapse. But a few still held out. By May, the last nine left the cave, because two others had died in there, and their decaying bodies were giving off toxic fumes! After checking to make sure that no one else was alive inside and removing the bodies of the two dead, authorities blew up the cave.

On top of their terrible experience in the cave, the cult members also realized that May 2008 had come and gone and that the world was still moving along just fine. Some of them probably felt very foolish, and by then, Kuznetsov, having been diagnosed with schizophrenia, was in a psychiatric ward. At least one member of the group remained faithful, waiting for the world to end. They're still waiting.

FAILED PREDICTIONS: POPE INNOCENT III

POPE INNOCENT III (1161–1216) was notorious for trying to silence critics and stamp out any threats to his church. For instance, in southern France a religious group known as the Cathars became very popular among the commoners, and even gained traction with some of the nobility. They considered themselves Christians, but their Christianity was very unlike what Innocent and the Catholic Church wanted people to believe in. At first, the Church sent missionaries to try to convince the Cathars they were wrong, using arguments and debates to prove their point. But the Cathars ignored them, and sometimes even won the debates! Eventually, in the early thirteenth century, Innocent III decided the Cathars had to be converted by force, or killed. So he authorized armies to launch a crusade against them (this became known as the Albigensian Crusade), bringing death and misery to southern France for several decades, and eventually extinguishing the Cathars.

Innocent wasn't just concerned with what was happening in Europe. For more than a century (since the 1090s), Christian Europe had been waging war against Islam over who should control the sites in the Holy Land, such as Jerusalem. Innocent and many others believed that the presence of Muslims in those lands was a clear sign that the end of the world was nigh. Various people tried to predict when that end would come, and many believed that the end of the world would happen—yep—666 years after the Prophet Muhammad founded Islam. In this case, that put the end of the world sometime in the year 1284.

People began to get anxious and nervous about this date. Many, including Innocent, the head of the most powerful entity in the West, believed it was really going to happen. The Christians losing their grip on the Middle East was only further proof that all was proceeding toward the ultimate end. As a sign of how revved up people were, a fight broke out at the University of Paris, with teachers accusing the Franciscan and Dominican Orders and their students of being agents of the devil, the very ones who would bring about the apocalypse. It seems ridiculous now, but many powerful people took the matter seriously, and took sides in the dispute.

And so, 1284 came … and went. And nothing much happened. In fact, in 1291, the Muslims finally expelled the Christians from the Holy Land for good. So in some sense, one world did come to an end. It just wasn't the one Christians in Europe were expecting.

FAILED PREDICTIONS:
THE GERMAN FLOOD OF 1524

IN THE YEAR 1499, a German astronomer and mathematician named Johannes Stöffler made a bold prediction: he claimed that on February 20, 1524, the entire world would be drowned in a flood, just like the one in the Bible, and all those other myths from the ancient world. He based this on various calculations about alignments of the planets that would happen during the water sign of Pisces, which appears in the zodiac from late February into March.

This was quite a shock, but to many, Stöffler was using what seemed like solid science to make the prediction. So people didn't just laugh it off; a whole lot of them took it very seriously. Brochures and pamphlets were printed and made their way around to many towns and cities, all telling of this terrible day when the world would end. The campaign persuaded a lot of people, and caused some strange things to happen.

The first was boatbuilders suddenly found themselves getting a lot of orders! These craftsmen were only too happy to make ships for wealthy clients, whether or not they believed anything would happen. In one of the more extreme examples, a nobleman named Count von Iggleheim paid to have a huge ark (like Noah's) built on the Rhine, with the idea of evacuating and saving himself and his friends and family.

Finally, the day of the deluge came. It had been a pretty dry season up till then, but sure enough, rain began to fall! Some people panicked. Many rushed and fought to get on board Iggleheim's ark. A lot of people were hurt, and Iggleheim himself was killed!

And then ... the rain stopped. Things got a little damp, but that was it. As February 21 came around, it was pretty obvious that the world wasn't going to end after all. People were relieved, some were disappointed, and as usual, Stöffler claimed that he had made a mistake in his calculations, and that the "real" date of the flood would be in the year 1528. Of course, some believed him, but as often happens when these things fail initially, a lot of people began to call him a fraud, and stopped listening. By the time 1528 came and went without the world ending, everyone was done listening to anything Stöffler had to say.

That dismissal is not entirely fair to Stöffler's soothsaying abilities. He did predict that he himself would be harmed by something large falling on him, and believed it so much that he tried to stay indoors as much as possible. But once, he had some friends over to visit, and when he reached up to get a book off a shelf, it fell on his head and injured him. Maybe he could see into the future after all!

FAILED PREDICTIONS:
THE USSHER CHRONOLOGY

JAMES USSHER WAS AN ARCHBISHOP in Ireland during the seventeenth century who decided to do what many before him (and after him) tried to do: figure out when Earth came into existence and when it would end. Shouldn't be too tough, right?

Ussher did this by delving into his Bible and trying to calculate dates based on the time between generations. After much study and comparing of chronologies, genealogies, and various other -ologies, he came up with an oddly specific date: God created Earth on October 23, 4004 BCE. He used as his guide the passage from 2 Peter 3:8, which proclaimed, "a day is like a thousand years, and a thousand years are like a day."

Because God had created the earth in six days, some reasoned that it would exist for a period of six "days," or more accurately, six thousand years. Ussher was by no means the first to come up with this idea, as others had also suggested that Earth made its grand entrance into the universe about 6,000 years ago.

This calculation made an end date nice and easy, too: shortly before or after the year 2000 CE. In that year, the incidents described in Revelation would come to be, Christ would return, and human life on Earth would come to an end.

Beliefs in the 6,000-year-old Earth lasted well into the nineteenth century, but began to be challenged when scientists started discovering dinosaur bones, and were able to date the planet more accurately using various methods. The idea that Earth was at least millions of years old began to take hold, even as those who believed Ussher and others like him pushed back. We now know Earth is about 4.6 billion years old. There is still a group that very firmly believes in "Young Earth creationism," and argues for its inclusion in science textbooks and other places, even though they have no evidence to support their theory.

In any case, Ussher and a whole lot of others were sure that the world would end sometime around 2000, a logical date based on their beliefs. More than twenty years on, we can see that the archbishop was not correct, but many still believe that Ussher and others like him were on to something, and that the day is just around the corner.

FAILED PREDICTIONS: NEW ENGLAND, 1780

SOMETHING STRANGE HAPPENED in the skies over New England early on May 19, 1780. At about 9:00 a.m., the sky began to darken, until it seemed like night had fallen. Birds even went back to sleep, and other animals were clearly upset by the event. There was no eclipse or other astronomical phenomenon at the time, so people had no idea what was going on. Some were very afraid, and yes, many worried that it was the beginning of the end of the world. Terrified, people took to the streets and tried to comfort one another. Was this a sign from an angry God that the Day of Judgment was here at last?

Thank goodness, it wasn't. It seems that the most likely cause of the darkness was ash from a far-off forest fire. We've seen this in recent years, where fires along the West Coast of the United States scatter smoke and ash far and wide, making the skies turn orange, red, or even dark gray in places nowhere near the blaze. This can last for a few days before it is blown out again by winds high up in the atmosphere. If there are clouds or fog in the area, these can trap the ash and cause it to linger above, adding to the gloom.

So, New England was probably experiencing something similar. By about midnight, the skies cleared and people said they could see the stars. The Day of Judgment seemed to have been delayed! But this didn't stop some religious groups from claiming that the darkness was a warning from God. One group, called the Shakers, had a very successful recruitment of new members after this event, convincing people that the whole thing was indeed a sign that they needed to repent and live better lives.

Most people, however, just got on with their lives and chalked it up to yet another one of those weird happenings New England is so famous for. One amusing story says that in Connecticut, the government was in an early morning meeting when the darkness started. Most of those assembled wanted to leave, assuming that the end of the world was upon them, but a man named Abraham Davenport said that if it wasn't Judgment Day, then there was no reason to adjourn the meeting, and if it was, he wanted to be seen by God as working hard and doing his duty right until the end. So he asked that candles be lit and that the meeting continue! Think you'd be capable of remaining that levelheaded?

————————————

FAILED PREDICTIONS: WILLIAM MILLER AND THE MILLERITES

WILLIAM MILLER (1782–1849) was an American Baptist preacher who gained quite a lot of fame in the 1840s for his bold and outrageous predictions. Miller had committed himself to studying various Bible passages with the idea of trying to see if they could be used to predict the future. He read Daniel 8:14, which says "And he said unto me, Unto two thousand and three hundred days; then shall the sanctuary be cleansed." Miller interpreted these days to mean years, and dated the prophecy from the year 457 BCE, when the Persian emperor gave the command to rebuild Jerusalem.

Using this day-year symbolism, Miller concluded that the world would come to an end soon. He wrote, "My principles in brief, are, that Jesus Christ will come again to this earth, cleanse, purify, and take possession of the same, with all the saints, sometime between March 21, 1843, and March 21, 1844."

As you may have noticed, when someone makes such a definitive prediction, it usually gains a lot of attention, and this is exactly what happened with Miller. Before, he had been an obscure preacher from New York, but by 1840, he was being reported on in national newspapers and attracting a lot of new followers, a flock that became known as the Millerites. It's thought that there were between fifty thousand and a half million of them at the movement's height. No doubt, many people were excited about his prediction, some eagerly awaiting, others likely very afraid.

As 1843 dawned, Miller's congregation held their breath. The year passed uneventfully, and turned into 1844. No matter, they said, there was still time, and it made sense that it might well happen at the end of the timeline Miller had provided. And then, of course, March 21, 1844, rolled around, and once again, nothing. Miller and some of his followers went back and recalculated, and came up with a new date: April 18, 1844. And once again, the day came and went without so much as a single horseman riding by. To his credit, Miller admitted to being wrong, but soon, another date was issued: October 22, 1844. This was it! After checking and rechecking, the date was set and considered final.

October 22 showed no signs of anything but fall weather, and by the next day, many of Miller's followers were no doubt confused. Indeed, the failure became known as the Great Disappointment, and thousands of Millerites abandoned their beliefs, feeling betrayed. Some joined other churches. But many walked away from any kind of faith. Miller saw his whole movement collapse, but he never gave up on the belief that the end of the world was coming soon. He died only five years later, still convinced it was about to happen.

The story of Miller and the Millerites is a good example of how people can get swept up by a single belief, so much so that they refuse to see anything else because they want so much to believe it. They are willing to support one another in keeping that belief going, even when it's increasingly obvious that they shouldn't. But once something comes along that pulls the rug out from underneath it, they feel lost, alone, and betrayed.

FAILED PREDICTIONS: MOTHER SHIPTON AND 1881

MOTHER SHIPTON WAS A FAMED MYSTIC and prophet in sixteenth-century England, who, like Nostradamus, made many predictions that people over the centuries believe have come true. She lived near a small town in Yorkshire called Knaresborough, in a cave with seemingly supernatural powers. The water in the cave has a high mineral content, so that things placed in it develop a buildup on them over time, which makes it look like they've turned to stone!

Mother's predictions were written down, collected, and printed in various editions over the centuries. In 1862, an edition of her sayings was printed with an astonishing verse: "The world to an end shall come; in eighteen hundred and eighty one." Given that this was only nineteen years away, this was quite a shock for anybody previously unfamiliar with this prediction! And of course, many of those people began to get very nervous. As the date drew nearer, some people took to spending their days in prayer, some abandoned their homes, some were desperate to make up for what they believed were sinful lives.

It got worse. Charles Piazzi Smyth, no less than the Astronomer Royal for Scotland, wrote that he believed that the Great Pyramid of Giza was built to prove that the end of the world would happen in 1881. He said that it had not been built by Egyptians at all, but rather, by biblical figures as a way of warning humanity when the end would come. According to Smyth, the pyramid's height, dimensions, measurements, and so on articulated a code that pointed to this outcome. Because of his esteemed position, many took Smyth seriously. Too seriously.

But, 1881 dawned. And passed. And nothing happened. It turns out, the editor of the 1862 edition of Mother Shipton's predictions admitted that she'd made no "genuine" prophecy about 1881 at all; this little poem had simply been put in there to scare readers and improve book sales! The book had scared so many people that the British Museum in London was contacted by a large number of people, all wanting to know about earlier manuscripts of Mother Shipton's predictions, to see if this 1881 prediction was genuine. It wasn't, and whatever one might make of her other prophecies, there was nothing about the world ending in 1881. A dishonest publisher just thought it would be good for business!

FAILED PREDICTIONS: HALLEY'S COMET, 1910

THROUGHOUT HISTORY, many have viewed comets as important portents. Some have seen them as messengers of doom, whereas others have viewed them as sure signs of victory, either during a military campaign or some other conflict.

Halley's comet is probably the most famous comet of all. Named for Edmond Halley, who discovered it in the early eighteenth century, Halley's comet orbits the sun, taking between 74 and 79 years to make one complete circuit (it averages about 76 years). It is possible to calculate when it would have been seen in the past, based on its orbital path and the time it takes to make that orbit. It was seen in 1066, the year that William the Conqueror invaded England and took the English throne for himself. Surely, those who experienced that world-changing event and saw the streak of light in the sky must have interpreted the comet as an omen.

The comet last appeared in 1986, and won't be in view from Earth again until 2061. Its last appearance before 1986 was in 1910, and that particular revolution definitely caused some panic. In keeping with comet superstitions, some saw its appearance as "proof" for flooding that had happened in Paris, while others feared that war was on the way. They were right, sort of. The terror of World War I was not far off, though it wouldn't start until 1914.

But the biggest panic came not from the superstitious, but from scientists. Yerkes Observatory in Chicago made a shocking and terrifying announcement in early 1910, when astronomers claimed that they had detected a poison gas called cyanogen in the tail of the comet. Camille Flammarion, a French astronomer, made the terrible claim that this gas would seep into Earth's atmosphere during the comet's flyby, and could potentially kill everything on Earth.

These announcements caused shock and panic. Many other astronomers were quick to point out that this was very unlikely, and that even if there were such gases in the tail, there wouldn't be enough of them to do any harm. But it was too late. People began buying gas masks and medication that they thought would help, and creating safe rooms that were airtight—how they planned to breathe in these rooms after a few days is anybody's guess!

Some people thought the widespread anxiety was all a laugh, though, and fearlessly organized watch parties on their roofs to see the comet in the night sky. As you've probably figured out, nothing happened. The comet made its flyby, and everything continued apace. A lot of people probably felt very silly, and Flammarion looked positively foolish, but otherwise, all was well. The comet returned in 1986, and everyone survived again, so it's a pretty safe bet that Halley's comet poses no threat to life on Earth, neither in the past nor future.

FAILED PREDICTIONS: Y2K

AS THE TWENTIETH CENTURY came to a close, a lot of people were eagerly anticipating the start of a new millennium; actually the new millennium didn't begin until 2001, but that's another story! Anyway, many started to fear that the dawn of the New Year would be a bigger deal than just having to remember to write the correct year on checks, reports, and so on.

This time, it wasn't just conspiracy theorists or religious cults claiming that the world would end. They were out in force, of course, but another problem was making even scientists and world leaders pause and take a closer look: the Y2K issue. Y2K stands for "Year 2000," and it suggested that an issue known as the "Millennium Bug" would become a massive problem for the world's computers.

Basically, in the 1960s through the '80s, when a lot of early computer code was being written, programmers often didn't bother to enter four-digit dates in the software. In other words, "1975" was just coded as "75," which wasn't a problem, as long as there was a "19" in front of it. But what would happen when these clocks ticked over to 2000? Would they be able to distinguish between the years 2000 and 1900? A lot of people feared that they wouldn't.

Why would this matter? There are a number of reasons. One concern was banks, which used computers to calculate interest rates, among other things. If their computers read the switch incorrectly, and moved from December 31, 1999, to January 1, 1900, it would mean that they would be calculating a hundred years out of date, which could cause a huge mess. Airlines that kept records of who was flying might have their data damaged, because the computer would be looking for information from a century earlier. Power plants had certain safety measures that were date-related. What would happen if the dates became confused?

Obviously, the solution was to switch all two-digit dates to four-digit ones, but that was a huge amount of programming work, and many feared it had been left too long to fix. Then the panic started kicking in. Books forecasting disasters like nuclear power meltdowns, financial data being wiped out, life savings vanishing, and so on began to appear. There was even a terrible made-for-TV movie that tried to dramatize all the things that would happen just after midnight on January 1, 2000. Although most people went on with their party plans as they would for any other New Year, a smaller number waited with bated breath, hoping nothing terrible would happen. Would the world's computer systems go haywire and shut down worldwide?

Of course, nothing much happened. There were a few glitches here and there, but overall, society went on without interruption. At first, many credited all the extra work and money spent fixing things, but it was shown that some countries had done almost nothing to fix the technical problems of their dates, and they had no more problems than the countries that did. So the end of the world was canceled, once again.

FAILED PREDICTIONS: MELTING POLAR ICE AND A NEW GREAT FLOOD

IN THE 1990s, a writer named Richard Noone made an astonishing prediction. He said that on May 5, 2000, the planets Mercury, Venus, Mars, Jupiter, and Saturn would be aligned with Earth in a way that they hadn't for 6,000 years. This alignment would create a unique gravitational pull on the massive buildup of ice at the poles, causing them to shift and parts of the ice to melt, an event that would unleash trillions of tons of water over the planet. The massive waves that resulted would submerge huge amounts of land, and end civilization as we know it.

Noone claimed that this had all been predicted long ago in ancient books and even by the pyramids of Egypt. He wrote a book called *Ice: The Ultimate Disaster*, which had all sorts of details and "proofs" about why this global catastrophe would happen, and how the ancients had tried to warn us.

May 5, 2000, came and went with absolutely no disasters whatsoever. None. Not even a baby one. Astronomers and other scientists who had been calling Noone's book nonsense were quick to say "I told you so." They pointed out that planetary alignments have no effect at all on Earth.

So, either Noone had made a huge mistake in his calculations, or he knew it wasn't going to happen and was just trying to sell books. Or maybe he really believed it, so much that he saw things that weren't there.

Noone's book is a curious mixture of ideas. He claims that the Great Pyramid in Egypt foretells this disaster, and apparently has a picture of Jesus on an interior wall that no one other than Noone has ever noticed. The pyramid also might be a gigantic battery, and various secret societies know this but have kept it to themselves to escape the disaster, with some of them possibly journeying into outer space.

As the months and weeks before May 5 approached, Noone changed some of his language to say the disaster would "probably" happen, or it "might" take place. It's all well and good to make bold claims about something in the distant future, but you'd better be prepared to stand by them. As end-of-the-world stories go, this one was pretty incredible, and when Earth amazingly failed to end, Noone had more than a little egg on his face. But as usual, there were claims of miscalculated times, and he had followers that stuck by him even after his spectacular failure.

Never forget, if something seems too crazy to be true, it probably is.

FAILED PREDICTIONS:
THE NIBIRU COLLISION

NIBIRU IS THE NAME of a supposed hidden planet, a "Planet X" that follows a much larger orbit than the other planets in our solar system, and has so far not been detected by astronomers. According to some conspiracy theorists, this planet will pass by Earth at some point in the near future, causing devastation and cataclysm.

There is a little bit of confusion surrounding the use of the name "Nibiru" for a hidden planet. A writer named Zecharia Sitchin first used the name for a secret planet, claiming that it was the home of a mysterious alien race that came to Earth in ancient times. He said that these beings visited the ancient civilization of Sumeria (in modern-day Iraq) and became known by the people as the Anunnaki, the gods of their mythology. The Anunnaki do exist in Sumerian myths, but Sitchin claimed that they had been literal beings from somewhere else, and that they had taught humans the arts of civilization, giving us a needed boost. Sitchin's views were believed by some and mocked by many others, but he maintained that the planet Nibiru was real and will return on its long orbit again.

Another conspiracy advocate, Nancy Lieder, decided that the mysterious planet Nibiru was the same as the one she had allegedly been told about by aliens. This planet was four times the size of Earth, she claimed, and on May 27, 2003, it would pass close enough to us that its gravity would cause Earth to stop rotating for a few days. The planet's poles would destabilize and shift (see page 132 for more on this phenomenon), and the planet's crust would move. The damage would be catastrophic, bringing an end to civilization and much of the life on Earth. Right up until that day, Lieder insisted it would happen. Except, as you noticed, it didn't.

Lieder then said that she had lied to fool the authorities; she didn't want them taking any actions to harm people (martial law, prison camps, etc.), so the real date was actually a secret that only she knew. She didn't give a new date, but conspiracy theorists offered up other dates, the most common being December 21, 2012 (see page 133). When that also proved incorrect, some said Nibiru would return in 2014, then in 2017, then in 2018, and on it goes. Even Sitchin distanced himself from Lieder, saying that "his" Nibiru would not return until around the year 2900, and wouldn't cause such devastation.

While this silliness was going on, astronomers kept pointing out that a planet of that size would be easily visible in their telescopes if it were near enough to us, and nothing was even close to something like it out there. Lieder and others would always answer that scientists were just covering it up, hiding the "truth," and so on.

Lieder, like many other end-of-the-world advocates, is pretty obviously a charlatan who just wanted notoriety. She kept the con going for a long time, and then tried to find other ways to keep it going. She's mostly retreated from the spotlight, thank goodness, but that hasn't stopped many others from following in her phony footsteps.

FAILED PREDICTIONS: HAROLD CAMPING

HAROLD CAMPING WAS A RADIO HOST and Christian evangelist who had an annoying tendency to predict that the world was coming to an end very soon. He first said with confidence that the world would end in 1994. When that failed to come to fruition, he went back and did some more calculations, and came up with a new date, which he promised everyone was accurate: May 21, 2011.

That day, he assured everyone, would be the day of the Rapture, when the faithful would be taken up to heaven, Christ would return, and Judgment Day would begin. The next five months would be a time of terrible suffering for those left behind, with a million or more dying every day until October 21, when Christ would cast everyone remaining away, and God would destroy the world and the universe, and a new era of peace would be ushered in. How did he come up with this second date? By adding the number of fish caught by Peter in John 21:11, 153 to be exact. Yes, each fish equaled one day from May 21. Got it?

Now, this may all sound pretty out there, and it is. But many people who listened to Camping's radio program took this seriously and did foolish things like selling their homes, giving away their possessions, burning through all their money, and so on. So when May 21 came and went without anything happening, people were rightly upset. Many had donated money to Camping. Some had ruined themselves. They wanted their money back, but Camping wouldn't budge.

He claimed that after doing further "research," May 21 had been the "spiritual judgment day," and that the "real" Rapture and end would still come on October 21. Why should he give back their money, when the message still needed to go out? Very clever, eh? This may have satisfied some of his followers, but not all. Also, scientists and nonbelievers mocked Camping with zeal, and did everything they could to publicize how foolish he was. Mainstream Christian groups were also angry with Camping, deeming him a false prophet that should be ignored.

And when October 21 failed to substantiate Camping's claims, Camping was truly exposed as the con man that he was. He later said that he was giving up prophecy, and admitted that he knew nothing about when the end of the world would come. He died in 2013, never having given back any money, and leaving some of his gullible followers completely adrift.

CHAPTER 4
LITERATURE AND POP CULTURE

A SUBJECT LIKE THE END OF THE WORLD is way too good for most writers and storytellers to resist. And more than ever, these apocalyptic ideas feature in our everyday lives, as uncomfortable reminders that our time here is finite. Yet, we seem to seek them out, eager for the next terrible tale. Whether they are inspired by religion, science, or conspiracy theories, countless end-of-the-world narratives have found their way into books, TV shows, movies, video games, and more.

To conclude this book, we'll look at a brief selection of these entertainments, which have been very popular for the last fifty or sixty years, especially with fans of science fiction, fantasy, and horror. These are the places where our imaginations can run wild! From the Terminator movies to zombie apocalypses, from asteroid impacts to deadly space diseases, from vampires taking over the world to aliens coming to claim Earth for themselves, it's all here, and more.

THE LOVECRAFT UNIVERSE

AMERICAN HORROR WRITER H. P. Lovecraft, who wrote during the early 20th century, created a universe unlike anything any horror writer had done before. Up until his time, most horror stories were about ghosts, vampires, maybe werewolves … you know, the usual monsters who inhabit so many books, movies, and nightmares. But Lovecraft came up with something very different and very new. He combined horror with a terrifying vision of a crazy and hostile sci-fi universe from which humans couldn't escape.

In his stories, Earth is a planet of significance to a collection of alien creatures and species who inhabited it long before humans appeared on the scene. These beings often have tentacles, many eyes, blobby bodies, claws, and so on. Traces of these ancient beings can still be found in remote areas around the world, and his stories often involve investigators or everyday people stumbling onto secrets they later wish they hadn't!

One Lovecraftian creature is Cthulhu (kuh-THOO-loo), an ancient being who has been sleeping in suspended animation under the Pacific Ocean for millions of years in a bizarrely shaped city. He is about a hundred feet tall, with a face that has a mass of tentacles hanging down from it (imagine a squid or cuttlefish), and large, bat-like wings on his back. He has many devoted followers, both human and nonhuman (including a fearsome species of fishmen creatures called the Deep Ones).

Although Cthulhu is trapped under the waves for now, it's known that at some point he will awaken, and his bizarre city will rise from the depths of the Pacific. Then he and his cronies will go forth and destroy human civilization, enslaving some and eating the rest! Cthulhu will then reign over Earth for millions of years.

Cthulhu is not the only ancient being that threatens humanity; according to Lovecraft, many other monsters and ancient gods would like to bring Earth back under their control. They are all bizarre, nightmarish things said to be capable of driving people insane just by sight. The characters in many of Lovecraft's stories realize that they can do nothing about any of this. They may be able to run, or even kill some of the minor monsters that serve these horrific entities, but in the end, one or more of them will return, and humanity will be doomed. In the Lovecraft universe, it's always just a matter of time.

These stories were shocking in their day and have continued to be very popular. Today, countless novels, short stories, TV shows, and movies have been inspired by Lovecraft's works. Some fans have even written stories about what the world would be like *after* the return of these creatures, which is not a nice thought ...

SOME IMPORTANT APOCALYPTIC NOVELS

IT SHOULD BE NO SURPRISE that the end of the world has always been a popular subject with fiction writers. They can let their imaginations run wild and dream up scenarios that scientists haven't even considered at yet! Countless books imagine ways that it could happen, with the following being some of the most influential.

The War of the Worlds by H. G. Wells: One of the classics of science fiction, this story has been a book, a radio broadcast that may or may not have convinced some listeners that it was real, and several film adaptations. The story is simple enough. It turns out that Martians are real and have decided to invade Earth. They have superior technology and it's not so much a "war" as it is a struggle for humanity to survive. But although the Martians might be able to wipe out humanity, they have one big weakness that they don't know about yet ...

The Stand by Stephen King: Considered by some to be horror master King's greatest work, this very long and dense novel tells a strange and terrifying story. In it, the military develops a deadly form of flu that can be used as a weapon. Unfortunately, it gets out and quickly begins to infect people. Within a month, around 99 percent of humanity has died. The few that survive and are immune have to try to build a new civilization. This complex novel tells the stories of those survivors and the supernatural villain Randall Flagg, who has created a dictatorship in Las Vegas where his followers worship him (King would later connect Flagg to one of Lovecraft's evil gods). King wanted to compose a *Lord of the Rings* type epic, but set in modern America.

The Mist by Stephen King: This is a novella about a strange event in a rural town in Maine. People wake up one morning to see a strange sight: a heavy mist descending on the town, covering everything in a fog so thick you can't see more than a few feet in any direction. It soon becomes obvious that this is no normal mist. Things are lurking in it. Horrible, creepy-crawly creatures that are hungry and looking for something to eat! Things that look like giant insects, or giant crabs, or squid, or some combination of all three, as well as other

things never before seen. It turns out that a research lab nearby was conducting experiments contacting other dimensions and seems to have accidentally blown a hole into another one, allowing the terrible things that live there to burst into our world. A group of survivors takes shelter in a grocery store, but they can't keep the monsters out forever. The book is obviously influenced by the writings of H. P. Lovecraft (see page 190), and it has a very unsettling ending that leaves us thinking the world just ends covered in mist and monsters. A movie was made, which is also very good, but somehow manages to have an even more depressing ending than the book!

World War Z by **Max Brooks:** Max Brooks is comedian Mel Brooks's son, but there's nothing lighthearted about this book. It's an ingenious story written in the form of reports from all over the world about how a zombie apocalypse started and what happened in various countries as people and governments tried to stop it. It's written after the event, so you know that the world didn't really end, but for a while, it seemed like it might! Brooks's novel is a fantastic read that is far better entertainment than many zombie movies out there, and gives readers a real sense of what it would be like on the front lines of a zombie apocalypse.

The Road by **Cormac McCarthy:** One of the bleakest books you'll ever read, *The Road* is about an unnamed father and son making their way across the ruined landscape of the United States, a few years after a terrible extinction-level event of some kind ended civilization. We're never told what caused it; it could have been nuclear war, it could have been an asteroid strike. Instead, the story centers around the relationship between the two. They are trying to get farther south before winter, and closer to the sea, where they hope there may be other survivors. But not all survivors are good. Some are cannibals that are hunting them. The book is about their attempts to survive and stay alive.

Lucifer's Hammer by **Larry Niven and Jerry Pournelle:** A classic sci-fi story penned by two big writers in the genre, the book details the excitement of the discovery of a new comet. As scientists begin to study it, they find that it will pass close by Earth, too close for comfort. Although they assure everyone that nothing will happen, pieces of the comet do indeed slam into Earth, causing untold devastation in the form of tsunamis, earthquakes, volcanoes, and other horrors. In the aftermath of the devastating events, the book focuses on small groups of people and their fight to survive and rebuild civilization, with no guarantee that they will succeed.

Cozy Catastrophes: This was a style of postapocalyptic stories that became popular after World War II. The idea is that although most of the population has been wiped out, one or more people were able to carry on with their lives pretty much as before. Actually, they did even better, because they didn't have the day-to-day worries of their old lives to think about any more.

Good Omens **by Neil Gaiman and Terry Pratchett:** We'll end this section with something lighthearted and funny. A funny story about the end of the world? Yes, and a very good one at that! *Good Omens* tells the story of the approaching apocalypse, and how an angel, Aziraphale, and a demon, Crowley, decide that they rather like the world and don't want to see it end. But what can they do against the power of prophecy and the Almighty? A lot, it turns out! This delightful book was made into an equally delightful TV miniseries, and both are worth checking out.

SOME MAJOR APOCALYPTIC MOVIES

JUST AS THERE ARE ENDLESS BOOKS trying to scare everyone with ideas about the ultimate end, an equal number of movies desire the same thing! There are far too many to make even a partial list, but here are few highlights. Some of these are also based on books, but their film versions are as famous, if not more:

When Worlds Collide: A classic film from 1951 that is based on a book, this movie details how Earth is in danger of being hit by a rogue star, Bellus. A scientist discovers this terrible truth, but of course, no one takes him seriously. Eventually, it becomes obvious that something is very wrong, and several nations begin to build spaceship "arks" that will take a limited number of people to the habitable planet Zyra, which orbits Bellus. With time running out and people getting increasingly desperate, the tension mounts. Then Zyra swings close by Earth, its gravity causing great destruction. And still, Bellus approaches, one world about to collide into another ...

The Mad Max films: These films are set in Australia, sometime after a nuclear war has devastated the world. The survivors form small groups that battle over food and water supplies, as well as gasoline and other energy sources. The films are famous for their spectacular chase and combat scenes, as well as the crazy futuristic/punk rock fashions the characters wear. Though they are action-packed and thrilling, these movies present a bleak and depressing look at a dying world where people are fast running out of time.

The Andromeda Strain: Based on a Michael Crichton book of the same name, this 1971 film tells the story of how a satellite has brought back an alien virus. The satellite crashes near a small town in New Mexico, and those that are exposed to the virus die quickly and horribly, their blood turning into powder. Scientists and the military learn that this disease has the ability to wipe out all life on Earth, so they begin a race against time to stop it from spreading. Do they succeed?

***Armageddon* and *Deep Impact*:** In 1998, two blockbusters about space objects crashing into Earth were released. *Deep Impact* is about a large comet on a collision course with Earth. A reporter finds out the truth and the president is forced to go public about it. A team of astronauts is selected to fly to the comet and destroy it, but they are only partially successful, breaking it into two pieces, one of which is set to crash into the Atlantic Ocean. In *Armageddon*, an asteroid about the size of Texas is hurtling toward Earth, and again, a team of astronauts are set to land on it and drill into it, so they can destroy it with nuclear weapons, or at least break it up into harmless pieces. But of course, things go wrong, and the drama, heroism, and triumphant music swell ...

Planet of the Apes: One of the all-time classic sci-fi films, the original *Planet of the Apes* was released in 1968. A crew of astronauts lands on a planet where hyperintelligent apes live in simple towns, and humans are more like animals and unable to speak. After many adventures, the lead astronaut learns that he has returned to Earth in the far future, and that humanity has destroyed itself, allowing the apes to take over. The film has spawned many sequels, including a complete reboot in the 2010s, which used the idea of a deadly pandemic sparked by a virus originally developed to treat other illnesses. Once it escapes the lab where it was developed, it wipes out much of humanity, allowing intelligent apes to take over.

The Core: A silly end-of-the-world film from 2003 that focuses on a secret military experiment to cause earthquakes that can be used in battle. As you might guess, the experiment has an unexpected result: it stops Earth's core from rotating. Without this rotation, Earth can no longer generate a magnetic field, which means that it will be exposed to all of the deadly space radiation that normally is deflected. Everything on Earth will die in a matter of months. So a top secret plan is hatched to send a probe to the center of Earth and set off nuclear explosions to restart the core's rotation (we *said* it was silly!). Meanwhile, the damage from radiation is starting to occur, including deadly storms and destruction. Do these scientists succeed? Can they make it back safely? Is Earth saved? You'll have to tune in to find out!

The Day After Tomorrow: Based on the book, *The Coming Global Superstorm,* this film portrays an Earth in crisis because of climate change. The warming has a bad effect on storm systems, and causes the Gulf Stream (a major air current that circulates from the East Coast of the United States over to Europe, and keeps the continents warm) to change its direction, leading to temperatures becoming much colder. This, combined with increased storm activity, causes terrible blizzards and snowstorms across the Northern Hemisphere, locking it into a new ice age. Dismissed by many as fiction, some climate scientists in recent years have looked at the science and admitted that it's possible for an ice age to begin pretty quickly if the Gulf Stream shifts. Could global warming lead to a massive global cooling? We just may find out ...

The Terminator films: These famous action films speak to our concerns about artificial intelligence and robots gaining too much knowledge and power, and rebelling against us. The idea is clever: humans in a bleak future are ruled by machines that seized control of Earth and wiped out more than half the human race. These machines have found a way to send one of their own back in time to eliminate the birth of a boy who will grow up to lead a human rebellion against the machines and destroy them. The humans in our time have to escape this terrible robot, the Terminator, and save the future.

The Matrix films: These stylish action thrillers gave us another scary concept—What if intelligent machines had already destroyed the world, and we are merely living in a simulation, thinking that ours is the real world? This fake world is the Matrix, and the machines that control it use us as batteries, literally, to keep it running. But what happens when a few people begin to "wake up" and realize that the world we think exists isn't real? Can humanity fight back? Or has this all happened many times in the past, and will continue?

28 Days Later: A man wakes up from a coma in a London hospital, only to discover that no one is around. He leaves and wanders through London, finding that it is completely abandoned. Only, it's not. There are things out there, terrible things that were once human but have been infected with a deadly "rage" virus that turns them into mindless, snarling predators that only want to kill and eat, like fast-moving zombies. The virus was present in chimpanzees in a lab, but was accidentally let loose, and infected much of the country quickly. Now the survivors have to avoid being captured and consumed while looking for other survivors.

2012: Of course, they had to make a special effects–heavy film about this mythical year. It's as wild and crazy as you probably expect it to be!

SOME NOTABLE APOCALYPTIC TELEVISION SHOWS

TV CAN'T ESCAPE THE CLUTCHES of the apocalypse, either. What's worse than seeing the world and all of us come to an end in a movie? Seeing it play out every week in a TV show, of course. As with movies, some of these are based on books or comics, but each has a unique and terrifying life of its own.

The Walking Dead: Easily the most popular of the zombie shows, TWD has been around for more than a decade now. It has spawned a spin-off series, *Fear the Walking Dead*, as well as other upcoming shows that either feature some of the same characters, or are set in the same world. The idea behind the series was pretty simple. Something, maybe a virus or bacteria, infected everyone on Earth over a few months, and now when people die, they are reborn as zombies within a few hours. Also, if the zombies bite a human, that bite will make the person sick and they will die soon ... and be raised up as a zombie. Obviously, civilization collapses, and those that have survived have to make do in a new and terrifying world, where the walking dead are everywhere. Some advice if you're going to get into the show: don't get too attached to the characters, as they have a bad habit of getting taken out by hungry zombies pretty regularly!

The Rain: A TV show from Denmark, it tells the story of a deadly virus transmitted by rainfall. A brother and sister, Simone and Rasmus, take shelter in a bunker, and when they emerge a few years later, most of the population of Scandinavia is gone. They begin a journey to find out what happened and see if there is a cure.

The 100: Ninety-seven years after a nuclear war on Earth, a group of young criminals and offenders on a gigantic spaceship orbiting Earth are sent back to the surface to find out what has survived, if the planet is still livable, and what resources might be available. They arrive, only to discover other survivors still living on the planet's surface, and a lot of them are very hostile.

Jericho: The people in the small town of Jericho, Kansas, see something shocking one day—a nuclear explosion and mushroom cloud in the far-off distance, maybe in the city of Denver. Something has happened, but they don't know what. They later learn that twenty-three U.S. cities have been targeted—but who did it, and why? Has the world come to an end?

Daybreak: A lighthearted look at a postapocalyptic world, if that's possible, this show tells the story of seventeen-year-old Josh Wheeler, who tries to get by in a world where all adults have been turned into "ghoulies," or zombies, by biological warfare. As usual, they're hungry and want to eat the living. Josh has to work his way through some funny situations while looking for his missing girlfriend.

Containment: In this miniseries that envisioned a terrible pandemic, a man is found to have a very dangerous and contagious virus, and quickly infects others around him. The authorities move in to quarantine the section of Atlanta he lives in and think they have solved the problem.

But soon, people begin to worry that there may be cases outside the quarantine area. Not a total end-of-the-world story, but one that shows people working hard to prevent it.

The Leftovers: On October 14, 2011, a mysterious and terrible event happens, in which 120 million people, about 2 percent of the world's population, vanish without a trace. This series follows those left behind and how they cope with what's happened. Were the 120 million "raptured"? What really happened? The world doesn't end, but society changes completely as people look for answers to the disappearances, and to the meaning of life. And yes, something did happen to those 2 percent; something happened to the whole world …

The Last Ship: The USS *Nathan James* is a Navy ship on a mission to the Arctic, with just over 200 people on it. When it returns, the crew discovers that a global plague has hit and wiped out 80 percent of the world's population. The only hope for the remaining people may be on the ship, which has two virus experts on board. The crew begin a race to try to save the rest of humanity.

12 Monkeys: A show based on a movie, *12 Monkeys* tells the story of how a deadly virus (released by a group of bioterrorists known as the "Army of the 12 Monkeys") wipes out seven billion people in the year 2017. In the year 2043, the virus still exists and continues to mutate, meaning that it will probably kill the few people who are left. So the survivors make a desperate attempt to change things by developing a way to go back in time, to the year 2015, and stop the virus from being released to begin with.

Snowpiercer: After scientists accidentally unleash a frozen apocalypse on the world, the last survivors live on a giant and superlong train (1001 cars!), the Snowpiercer, that endlessly circles Earth. This show was a film before it was a series, and a graphic novel initially. It focuses more on what human survivors living in the train actually *do*, and a lot of it is meant to comment on our current social condition. Some residents want to hoard everything for themselves, for example, and those that don't have nearly as much don't like this at all.

Van Helsing: This show combines two apocalyptic events, an eruption at Yellowstone and vampires! When the supervolcano at Yellowstone erupts, it covers Earth in a blanket of ash, which blots out the sunlight enough that the world's vampires can come out during the day. The hero, Vanessa Van Helsing, leads a group of humans to try to fight back. It also turns out that her rare blood type can turn vampires back into humans, something vampires definitely don't want to happen!

Revolution: In 2012, an event known as the Blackout happens. Basically, all of the world's electronics, power grids, computer systems, and so on go off-line and can't be brought back, pushing humanity back to a more primitive way of life. In 2027, one family learns that they may have something that will explain why it happened ...

The Last Man on Earth: Another apocalyptic comedy, Phil Miller finds himself possibly the only man left alive after a deadly disease kills most people in 2019. He thinks he's all alone, but he discovers that at least one other person, Carol Pilbasian, is also alive and well in Tucson, Arizona. And then they discover more. And more. And it's all kind of funny.

POSTAPOCALYPTIC VIDEO GAMES

VIDEO GAMES ARE THE PERFECT PLACE to try out what living in the world may be like after life as we know it ends. Whether it's zombies, mutants, aliens, or demons, there is no lack of games that let you shoot, or otherwise take out, the monsters and bad guys that swarmed over the planet once civilization fell. It's almost like you have a duty to do something! Here is just a tiny sample of the games available; some of these are insanely violent and bloody, which you would expect if you're fighting demons and zombies, so beware:

Doom: Demons from hell found a way onto a base on Mars, and your character, a rugged space soldier, has to go through each level and clear them of monsters in increasingly violent ways. It was all good fun wiping out demons, but at the end of the game, after you've "won," a portal opens to Earth, revealing that ... the demons are here now, too, and have wiped out much of civilization. It's time to get your weapons together, go take out more demons, and save the world! This led to the just as popular *Doom 2*.

The *Fallout* games: This series has been running since the 1990s. Set in the twenty-second and twenty-third centuries, the stories usually involve a survivor searching for supplies and other essential equipment while traveling through a dangerous, post-nuclear apocalypse landscape (the war happened back in the year 2077). Oh, and avoiding strange mutants and monsters, or killing them!

Rage 2: In this violent, first-person shooter game, the player is Walker, the Ranger of Vineland, who fights mutants and other nasties in a world that was hit by an asteroid, 99942 Apophis (which is a real asteroid, by the way, that will pass by Earth very closely in a few decades). This game imagines what might happen if that ever did happen. It's not pretty, so let's hope it never happens!

The *State of Decay* games: Set in a fictional place called Trumbull Valley, you return after a fishing trip to discover that a zombie plague has broken out! The U.S. Army is already there, but not to help; they want to make sure that the plague doesn't spread. So, you're on your own in terms of fighting it. At the end of the first game, you realize that the zombies have spread beyond your area. Uh oh ...

Horizon Zero Dawn: Set in the thirty-first century, this is a fantasy/ science fiction game where the hero is a young woman named Aloy. She sets out to find out who she is and more about her world's history, and has to travel across a dangerous landscape to do so. The world is populated by large robots, simply called "the machines." Many of them leave people alone ... but not all of them. Aloy learns that the old world (our world) was destroyed 1,000 years ago, and then things get complicated.

XCOM 2: This sequel to a game about an alien invasion asks the questions: What if the aliens won? And what if people are starting to get used to the aliens being here, thinking they really want peace? But you know that they are really evil and desperate to exploit us. So, what are you going to do about it?

The *Resident Evil* games: A classic series of postapocalyptic games, the first appeared in 1996, and many give it credit for making zombies cool again! In this game series, you fight a whole bunch of awful zombies and other monsters, mostly created by the Umbrella Corporation, who developed a special virus for use in biological warfare. Only, it gets misused and starts making monsters! The first outbreak occurs in Raccoon City, and it's up to you to contain it before things get much worse. But a whole series of video game sequels proves that your efforts are futile ...

THE END?

FOR AS LONG AS WE'VE BEEN AROUND, we've wondered about our planet and our universe: where it comes from, where it's going, and where it will take us. Not every culture around the world has a belief in the end of all things, but as you can see from these stories, many do, and conceiving an ultimate end has been an important part of many ideologies. Beliefs, myths, and legends all contribute to the way a group of people view themselves, and anxieties about the end of the world inform that definition considerably.

We know from science that Earth will come to an end someday, whether via our sun or some other astronomical cause. We also know that we, meaning humanity, will probably be gone long before that happens. In fact, there's a chance it may happen soon, as many dangers right now could bring the human species to an abrupt end.

But there are plenty of hysterical conspiracy theories and predictions about our fast-approaching doom, and as we've seen, most of these can just be ignored. If something sounds too crazy to be true, it probably is, and you can sleep easier knowing that it's all just nonsense. As it stands, not a one of these predictions has ever come true.

Although it's right to wonder about where we're headed and worry about things that could harm our planet and our civilization, we also need to keep cool heads and not get carried away, as this book is filled with horrible tales about what can happen when an apocalyptic idea takes hold of a group of people. One way to keep things in perspective: keep rereading this book!

ABOUT THE AUTHOR

Tim Rayborn has written a large number of books and magazine articles about the strange and unusual, especially in subjects such as music, the arts, and history; he will no doubt write more. He lived in England for many years and studied at the University of Leeds, which means he likes to pretend that he knows what he's talking about.

He's also an almost-famous musician who plays dozens of unusual instruments from all over the world that most people have never heard of and usually can't pronounce. He has appeared on more than forty recordings, and his musical wanderings and tours have taken him across the U.S., all over Europe, to Canada and Australia, and to such romantic locations as Marrakech, Istanbul, Renaissance chateaux, medieval churches, and high school gymnasiums.

He currently lives in Northern California with many books, recordings, and instruments, and a sometimes demanding cat. He's pretty enthusiastic about cooking excellent food. To find out more about Tim and his work, visit timrayborn.com.

ABOUT CIDER MILL PRESS
BOOK PUBLISHERS

Good ideas ripen with time. From seed to harvest, Cider Mill
Press brings fine reading, information, and entertainment
together between the covers of its creatively crafted books. Our
Cider Mill bears fruit twice a year, publishing a new crop of
titles each spring and fall.

"Where Good Books Are Ready for Press"

VISIT US ONLINE AT
cidermillpress.com

OR WRITE TO US AT
PO Box 454
12 Spring St.
Kennebunkport, Maine 04046